COLORFUL QUOTES

40 INSPIRING COLORING PATTERNS FOR ADULTS

PETER MORGAN

© 2016 by Peter Morgan

ISBN: 978-1535150040

FIRST PRINTING, 2016

COLORFUL QUOTES

40 INSPIRING COLORING PATTERNS FOR ADULTS

PETER MORGAN

WELCOME

We all need to disconnect from our busy and noisy world sometimes.

Grab your favourite coloring pens or pencils, find a quiet spot and inspire yourself by coloring these playful designs.

Enjoy the relaxed state of mind that follows!

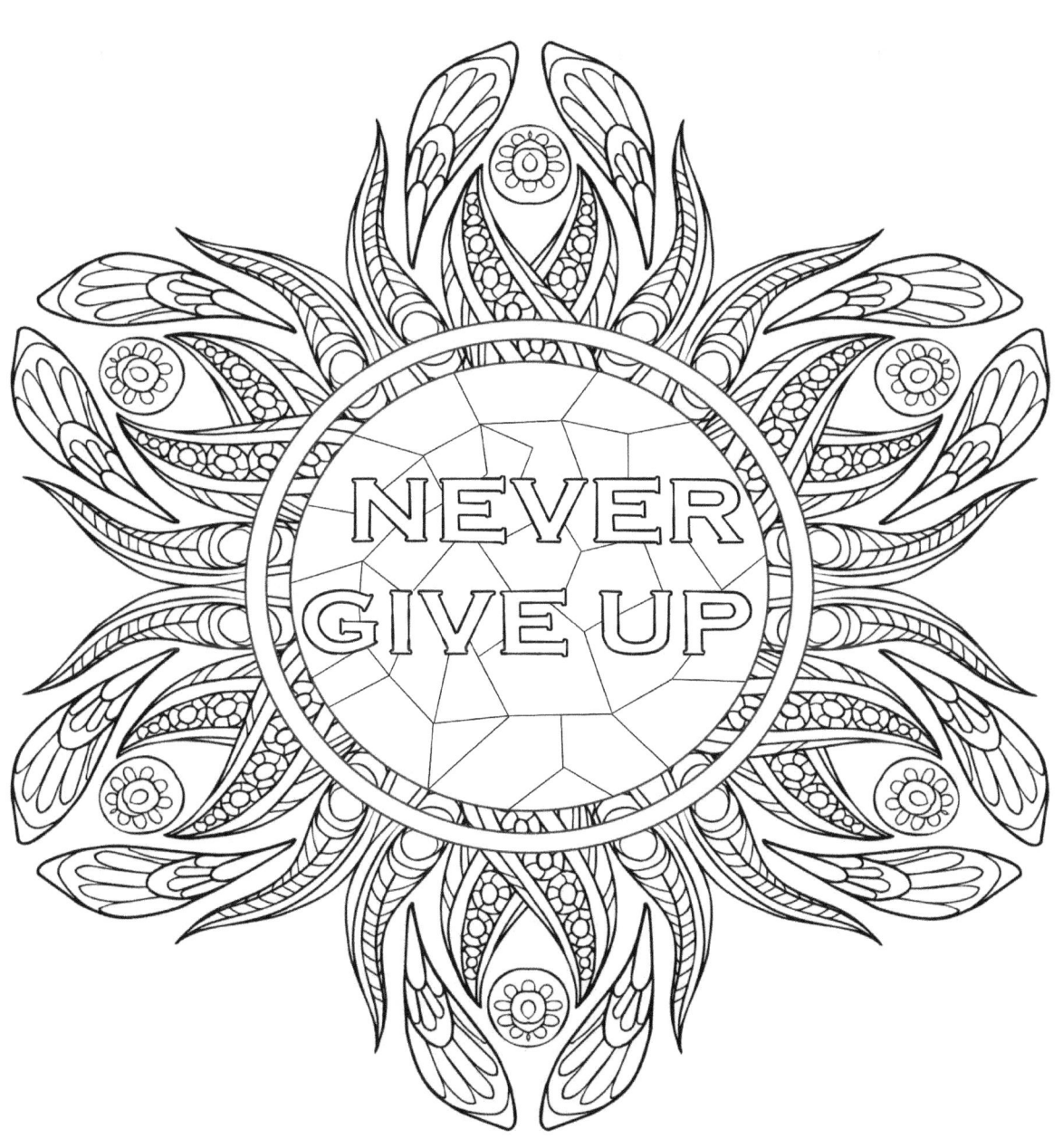

We accept

the love

we think

we deserve.

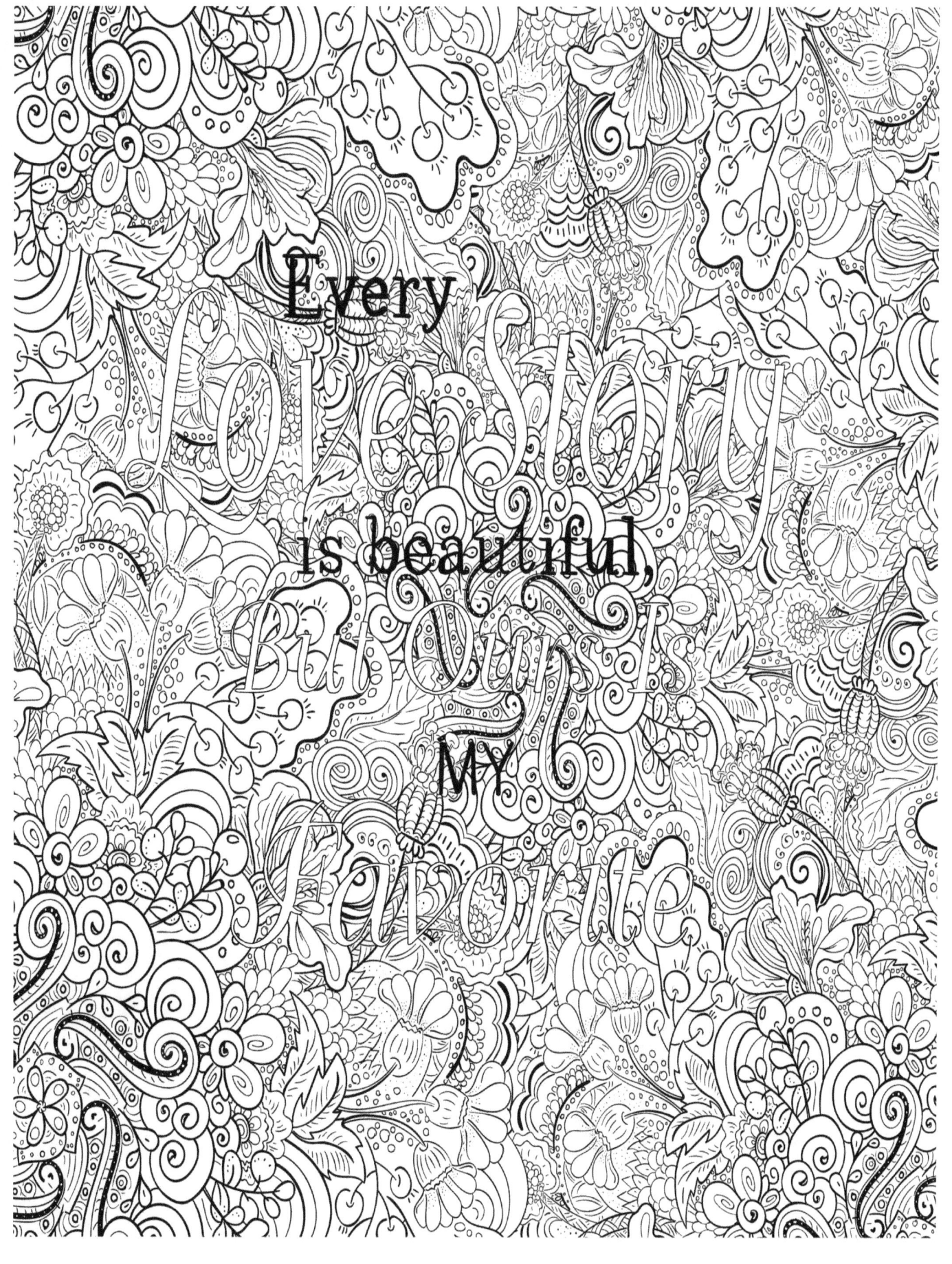

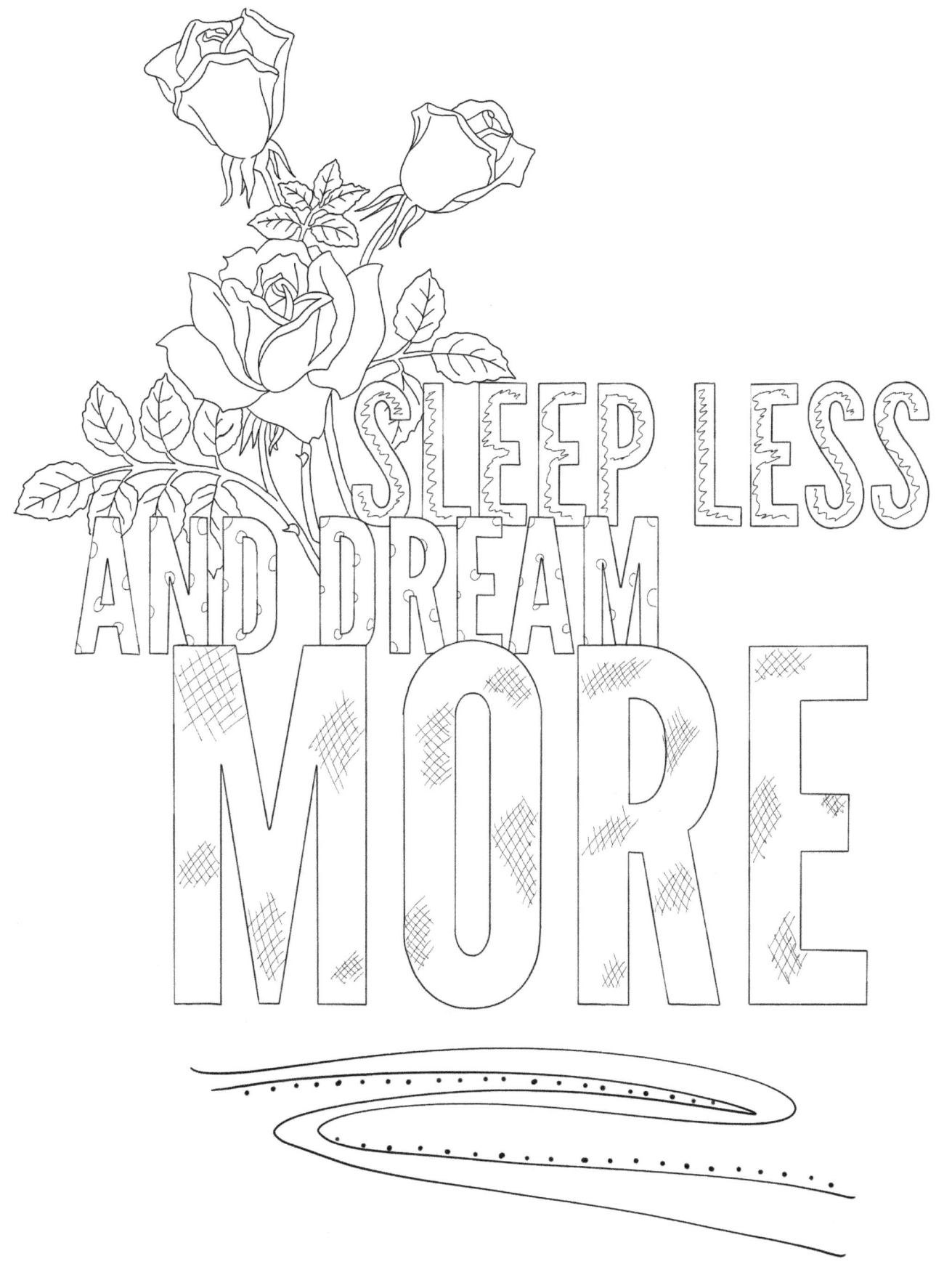

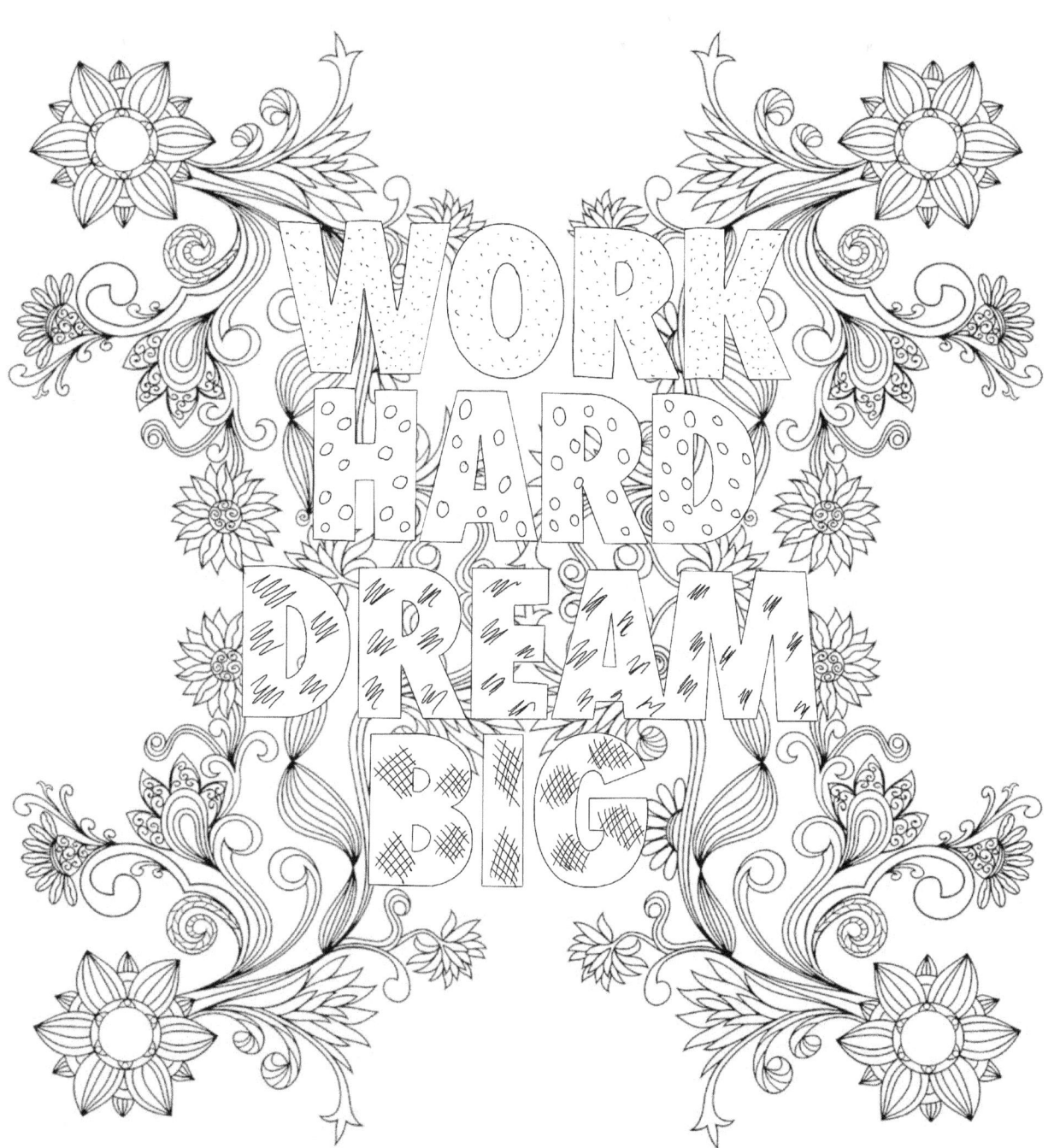

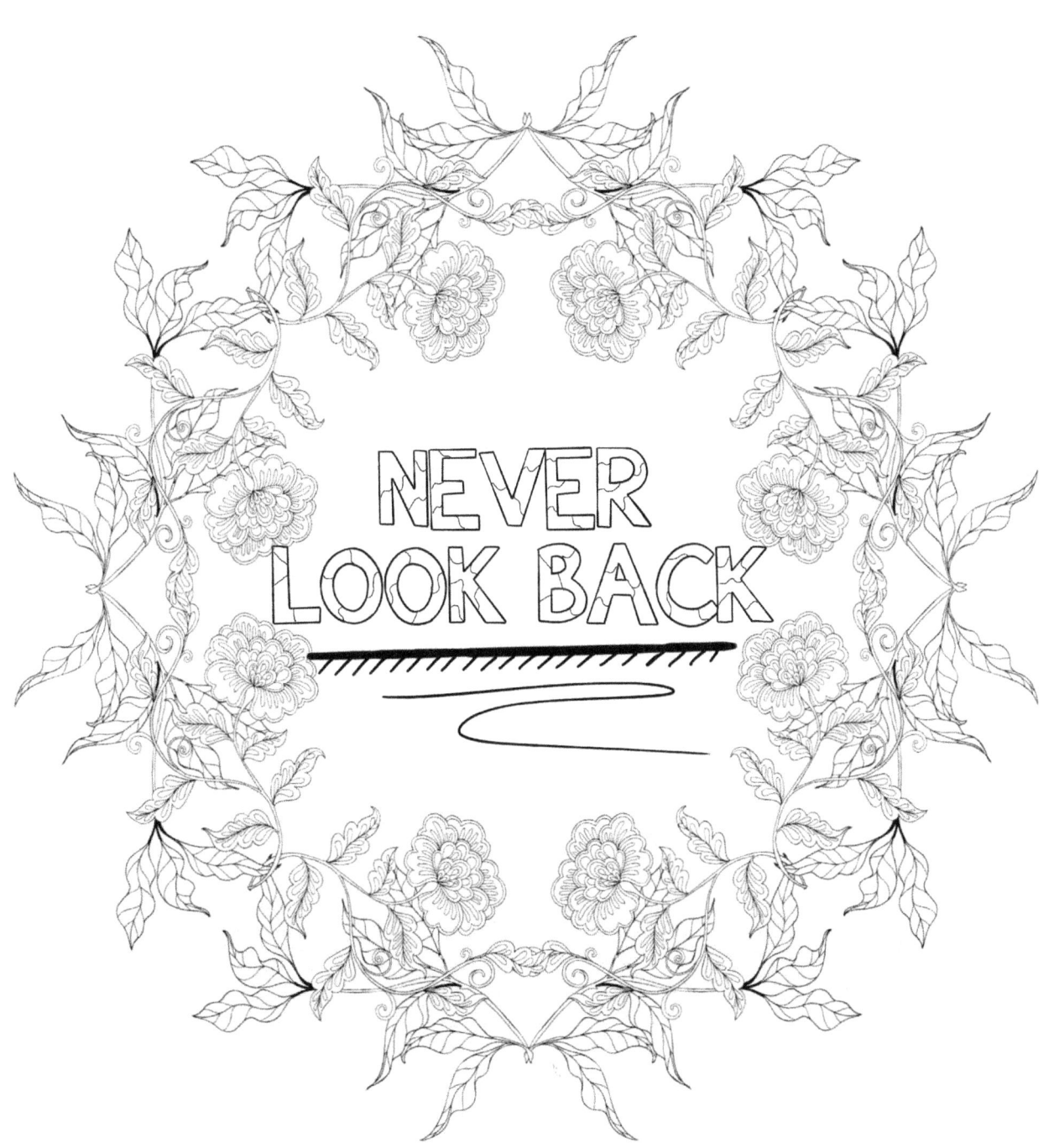

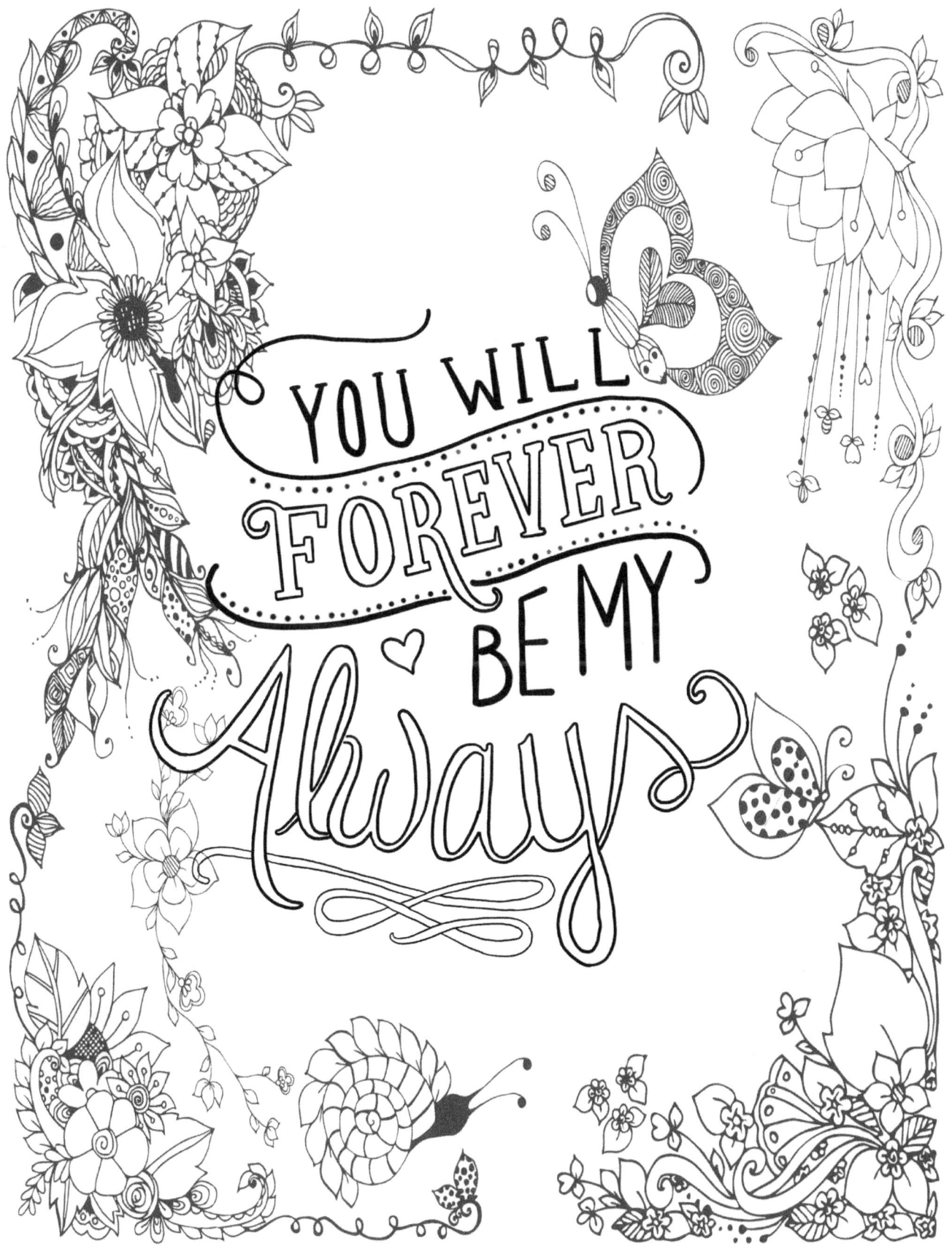

Music

IS A SAFE

KIND OF HIGH

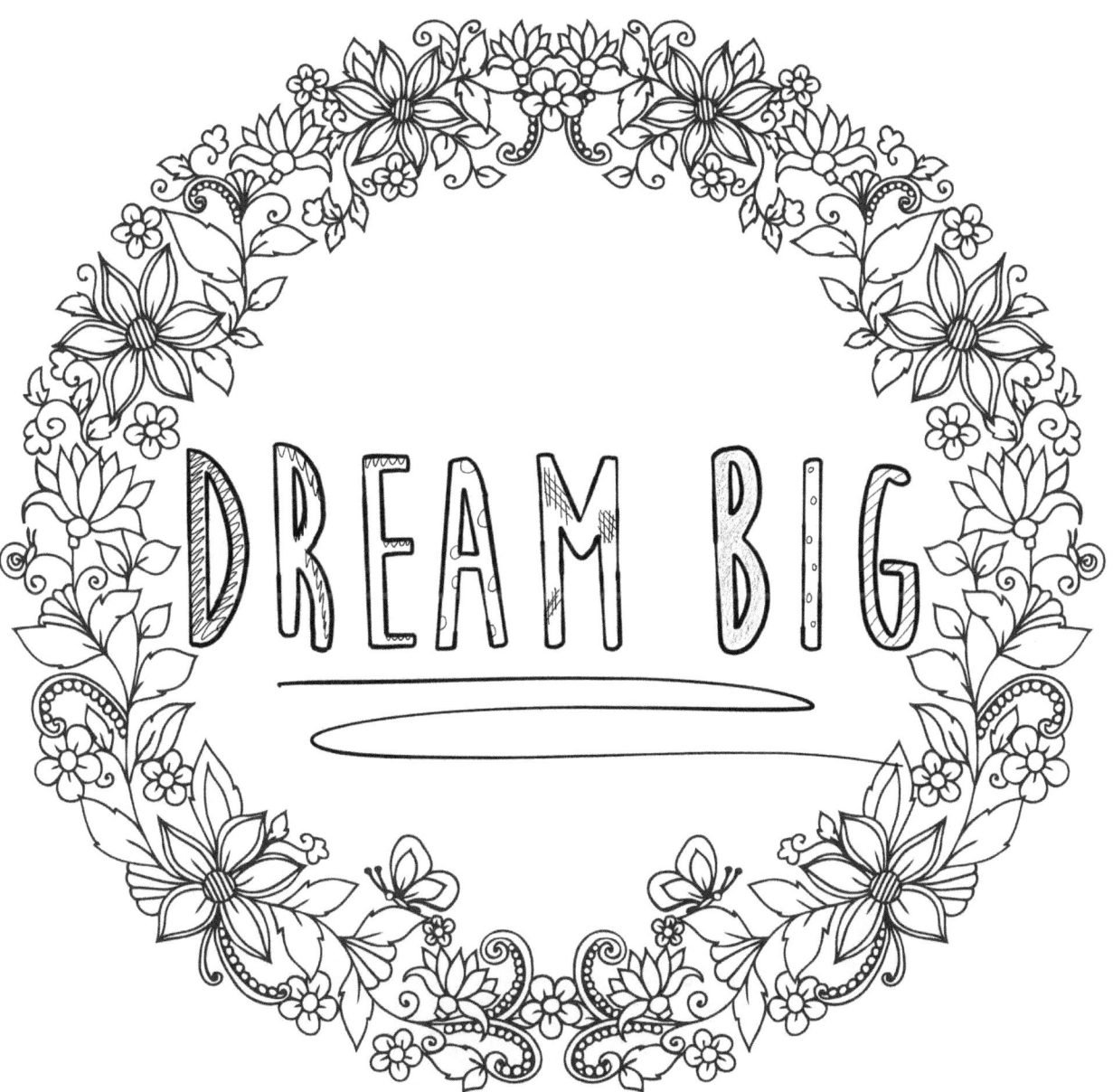

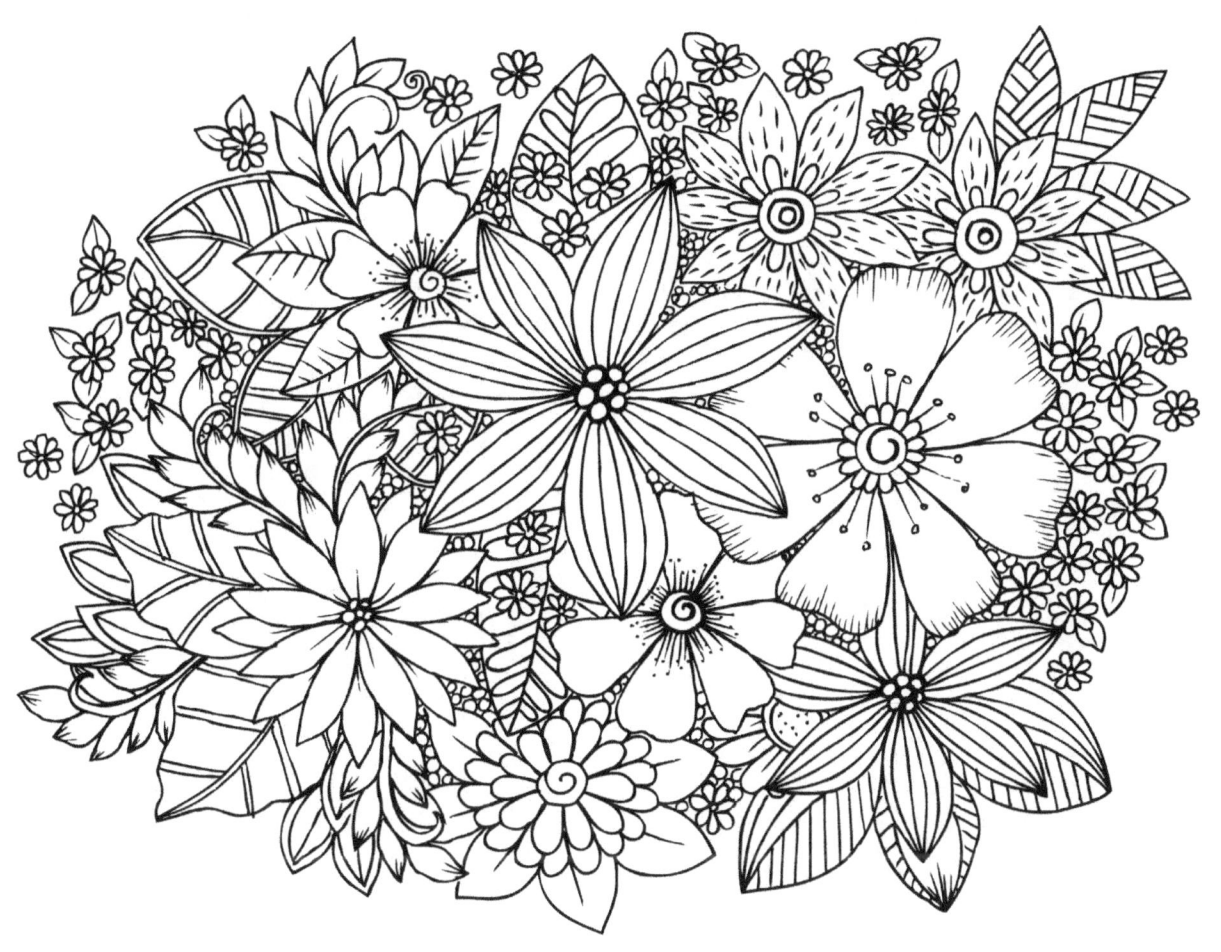

I was reminded that
my blood type is
Be Positive

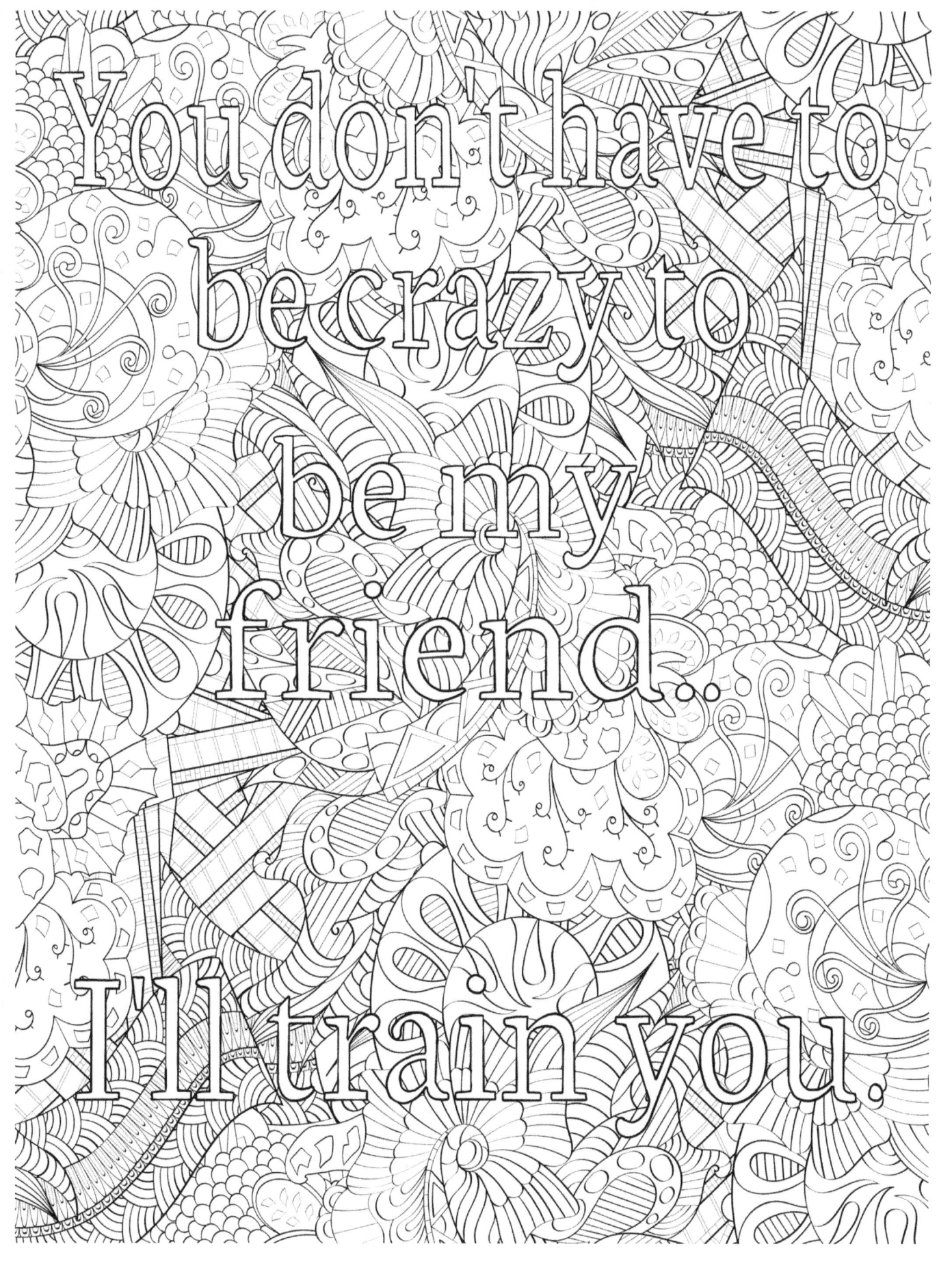

You don't have to be crazy to be my friend... I'll train you.

Do good and good will come to you

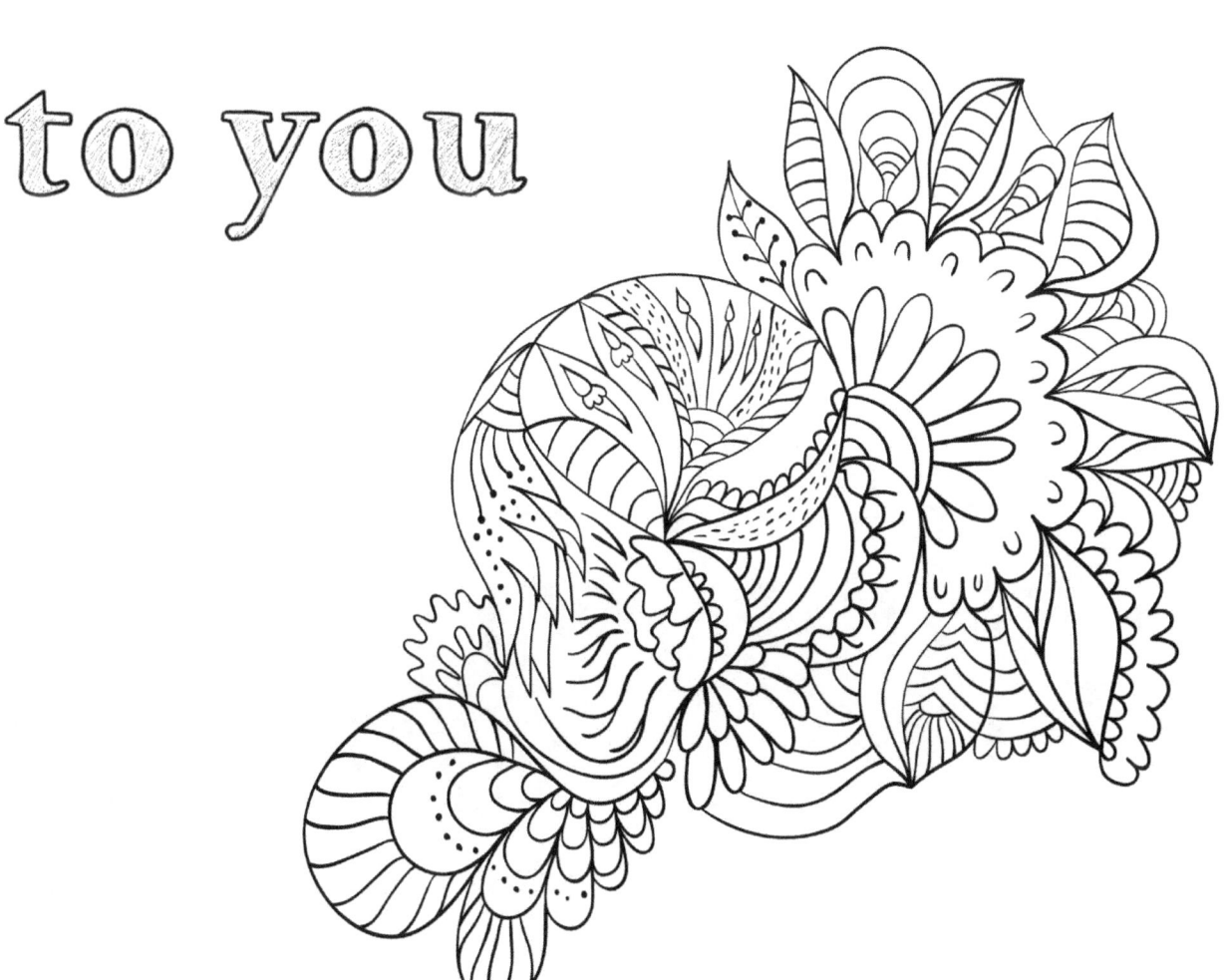

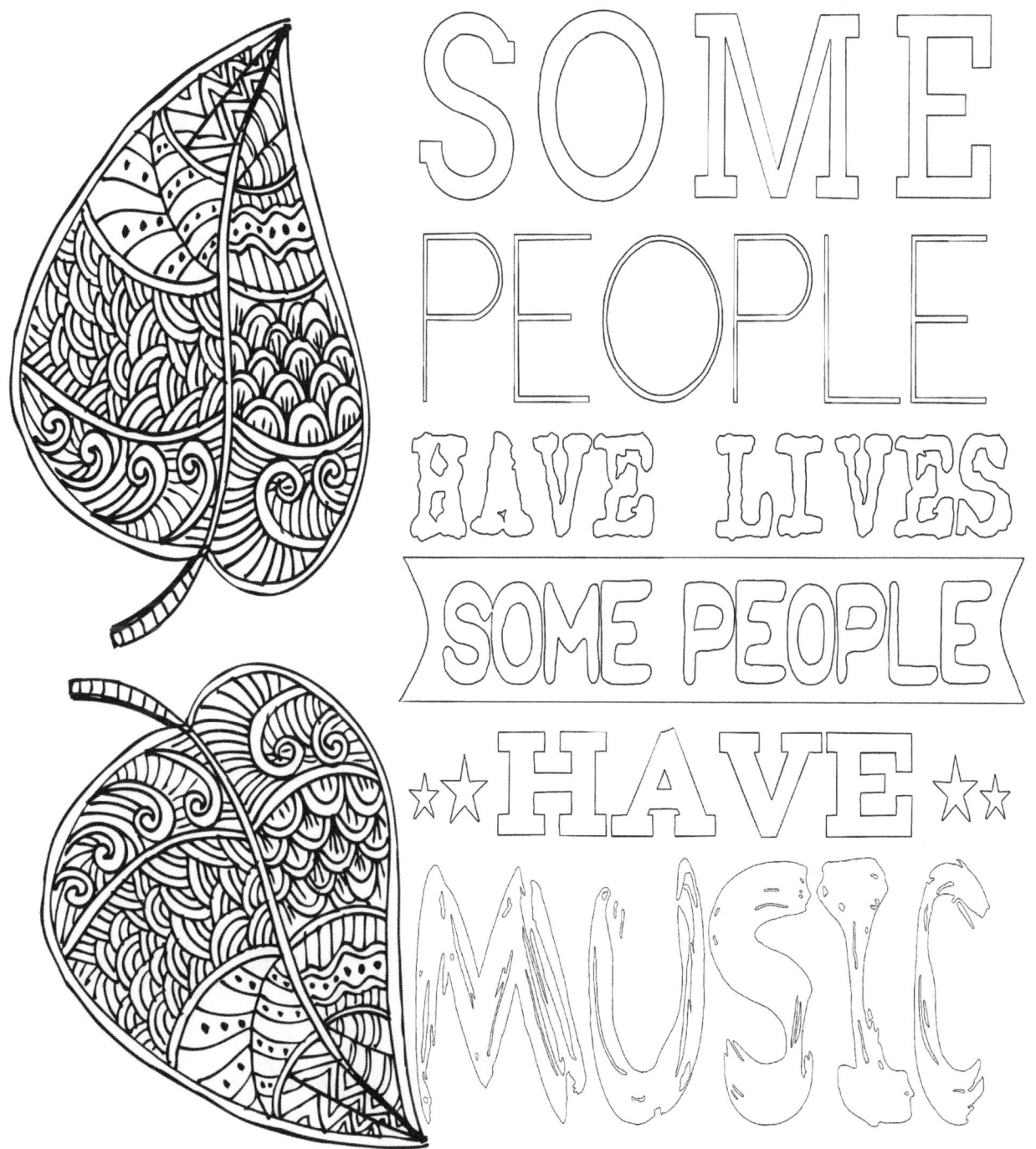

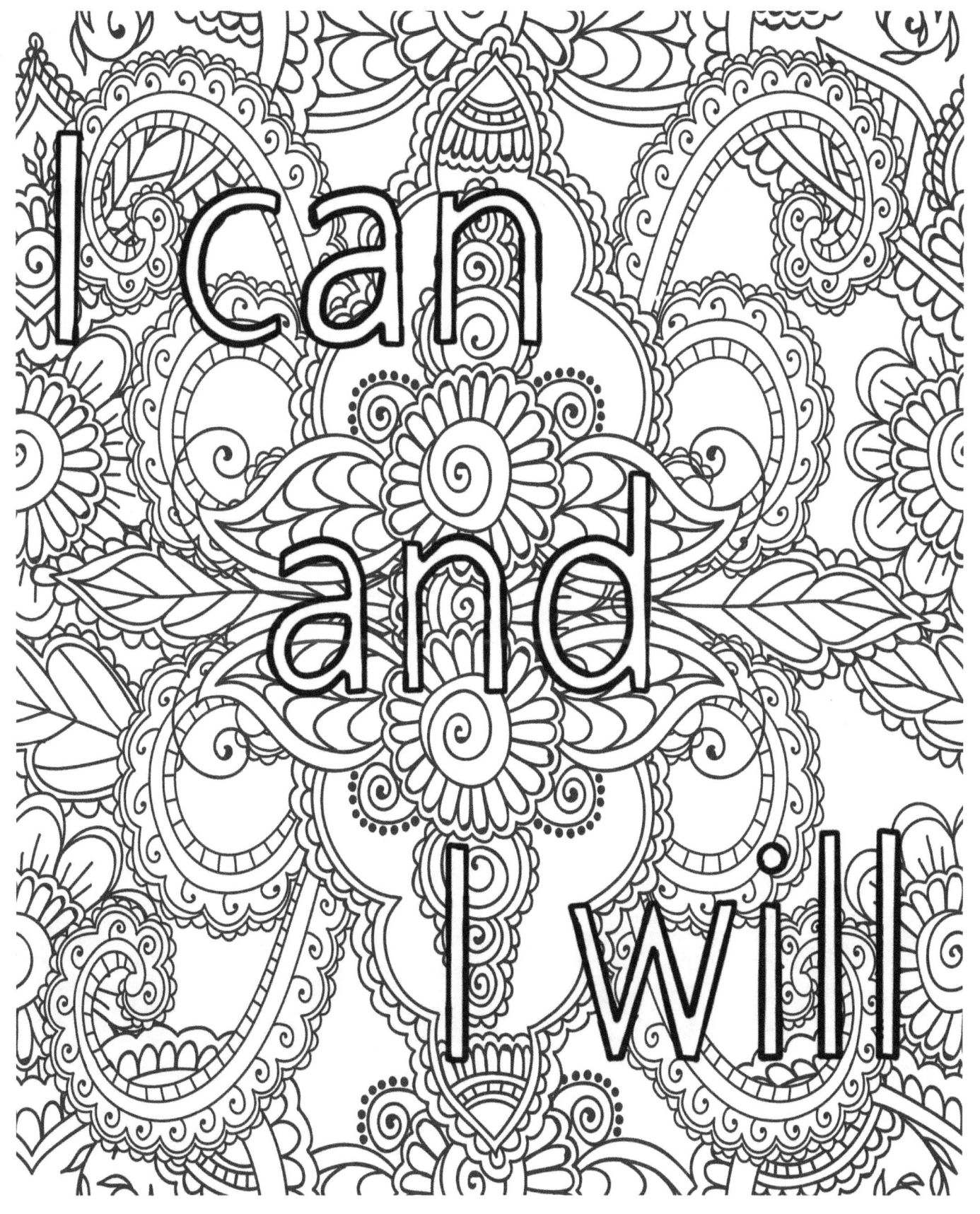

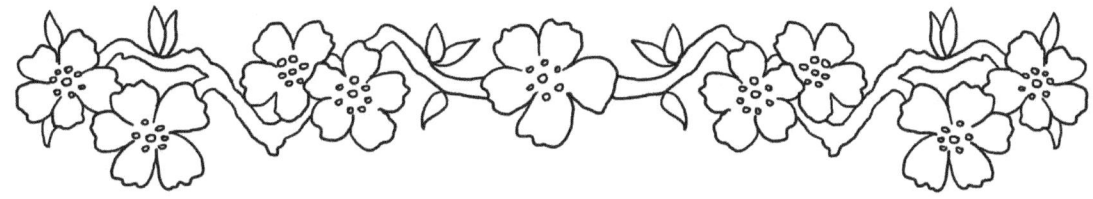

PROVE

THEM

WRONG

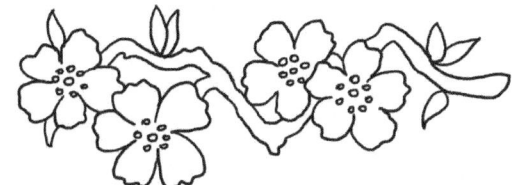 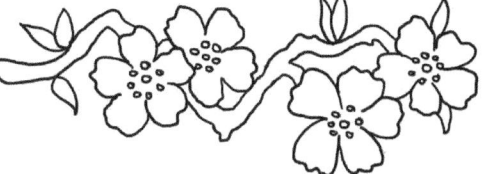

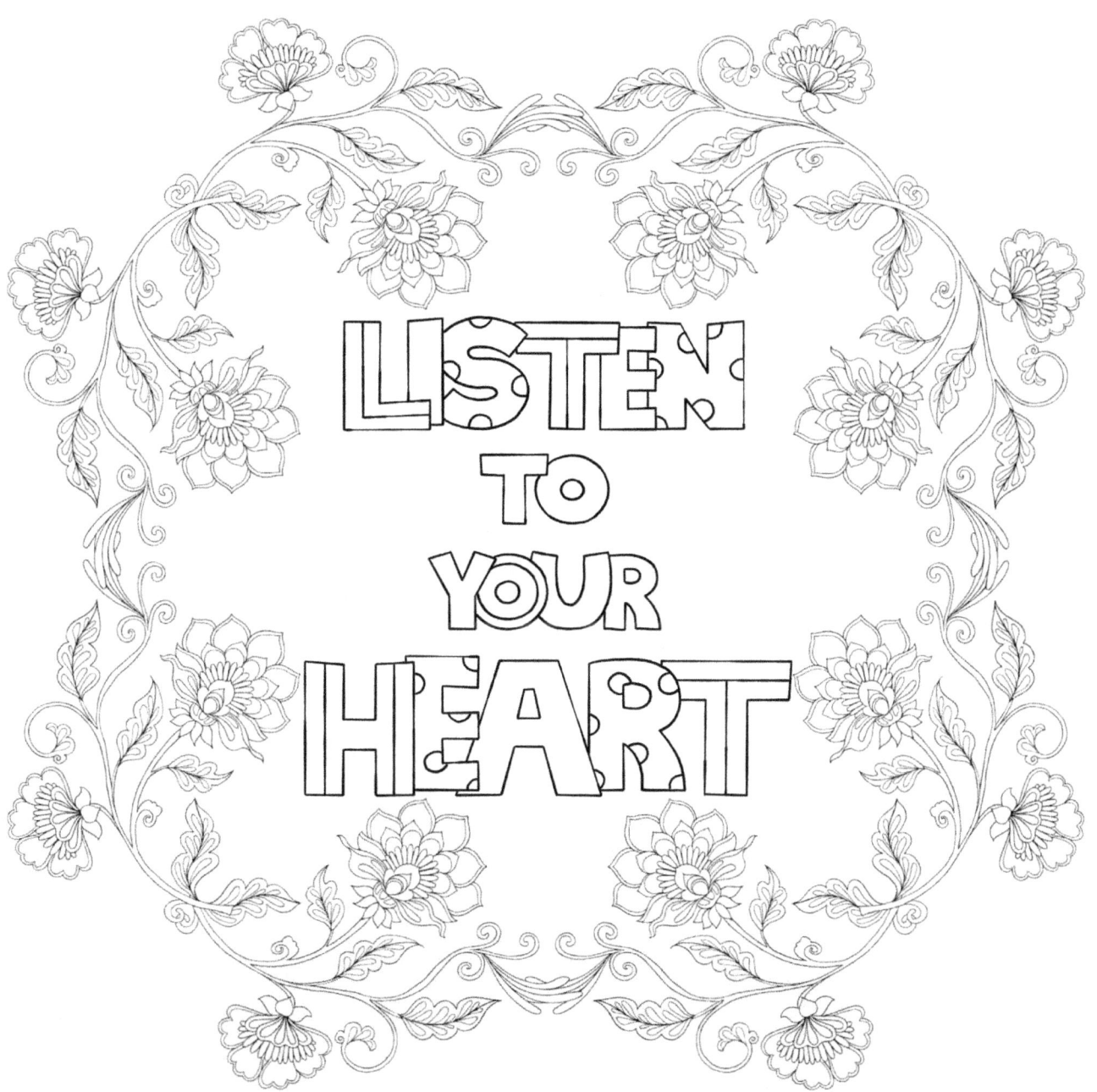

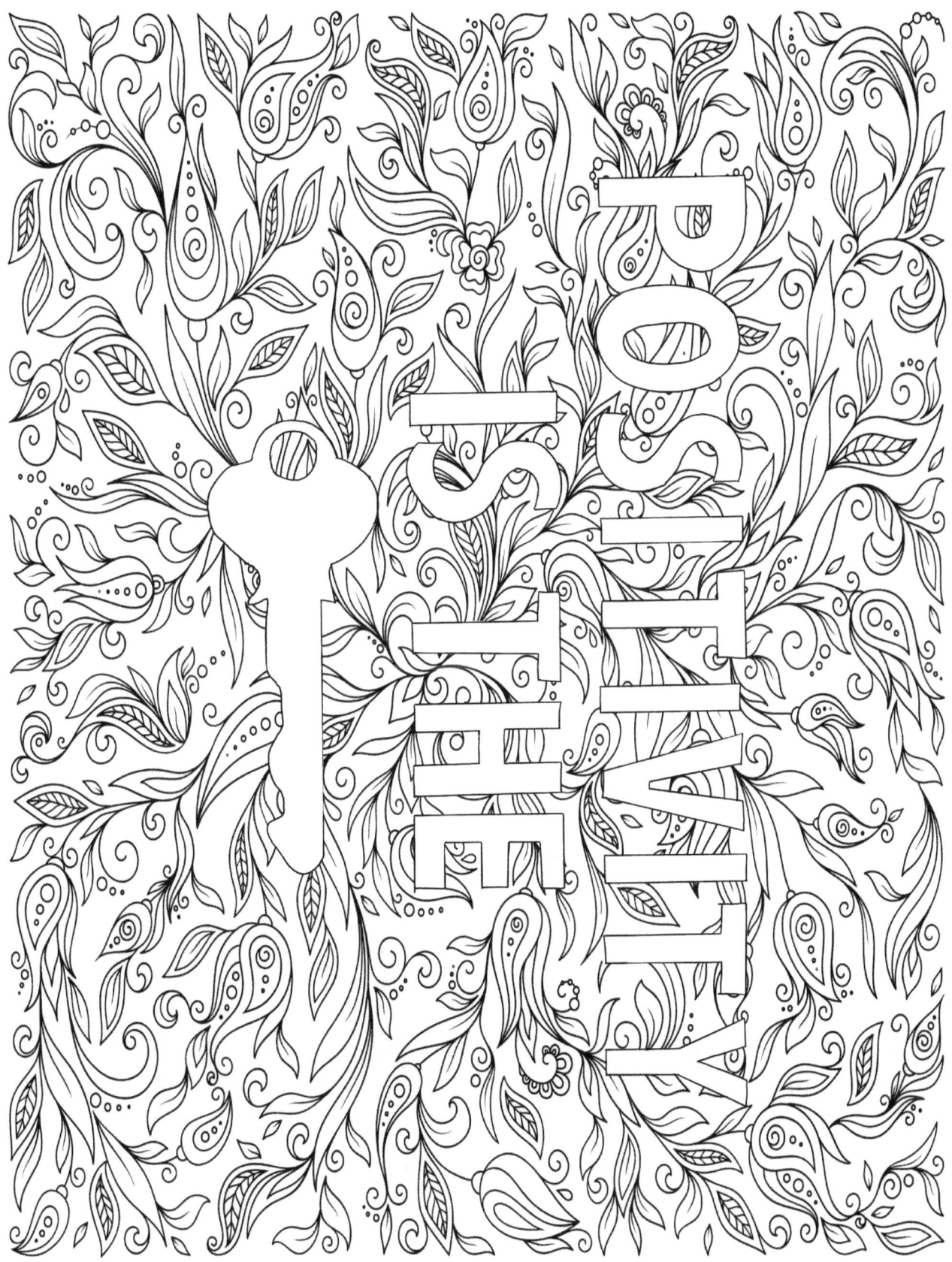

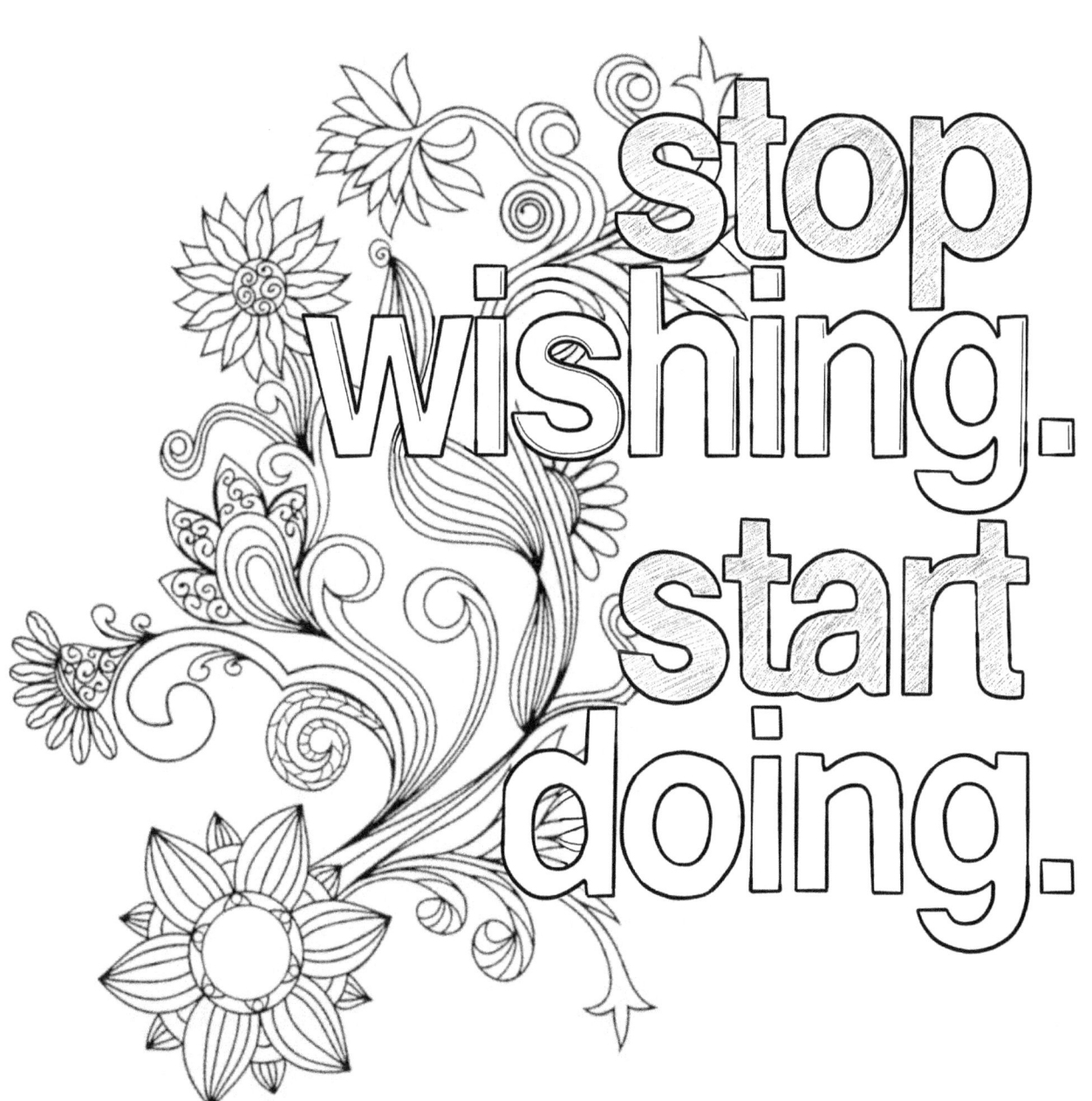

MAYBE OUR MISTAKES
ARE WHAT MAKE OUR

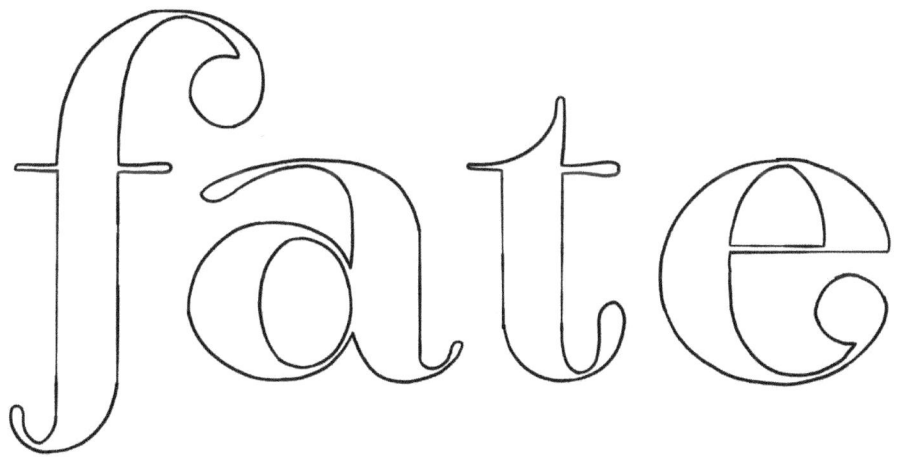

fate

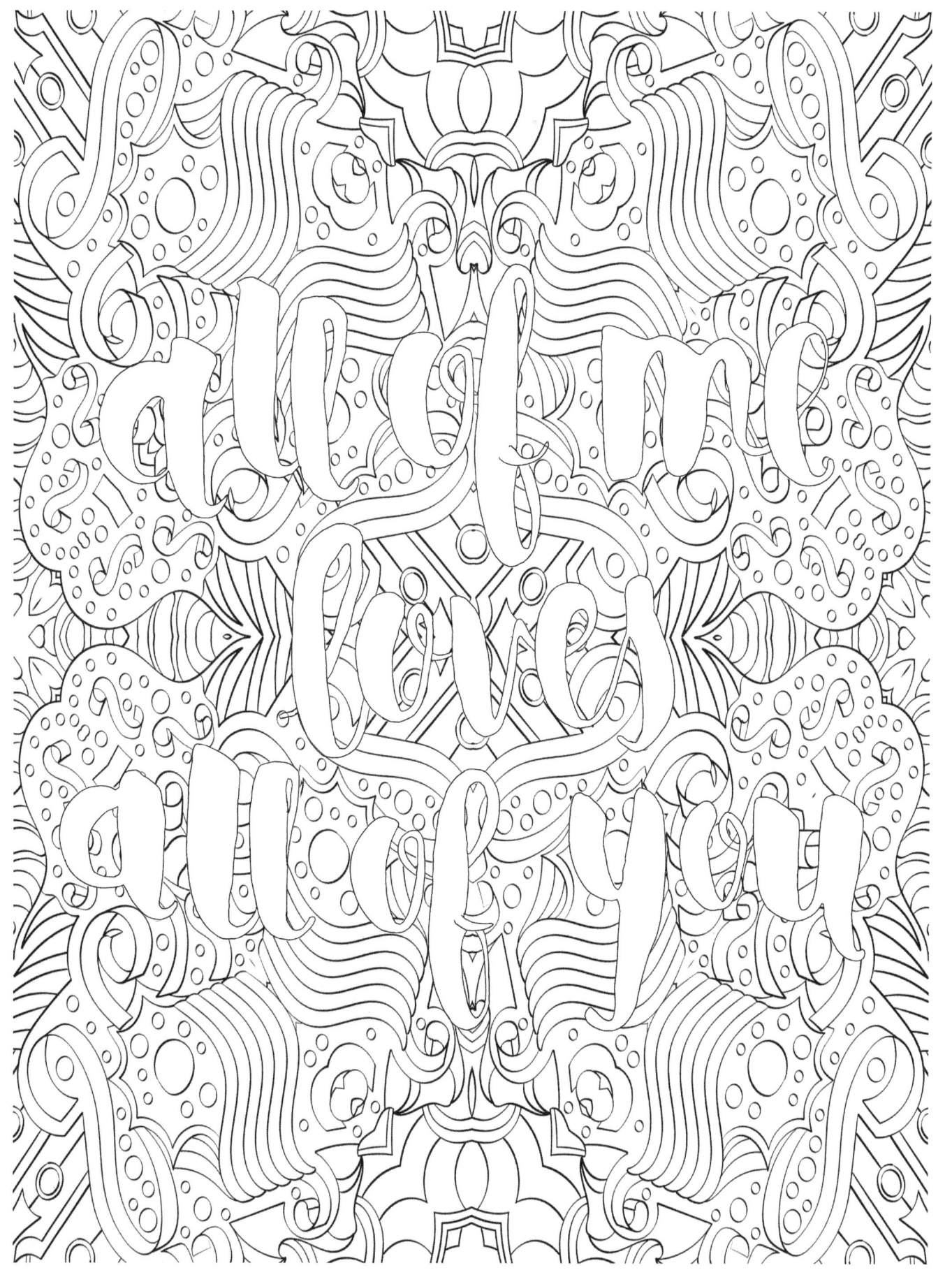

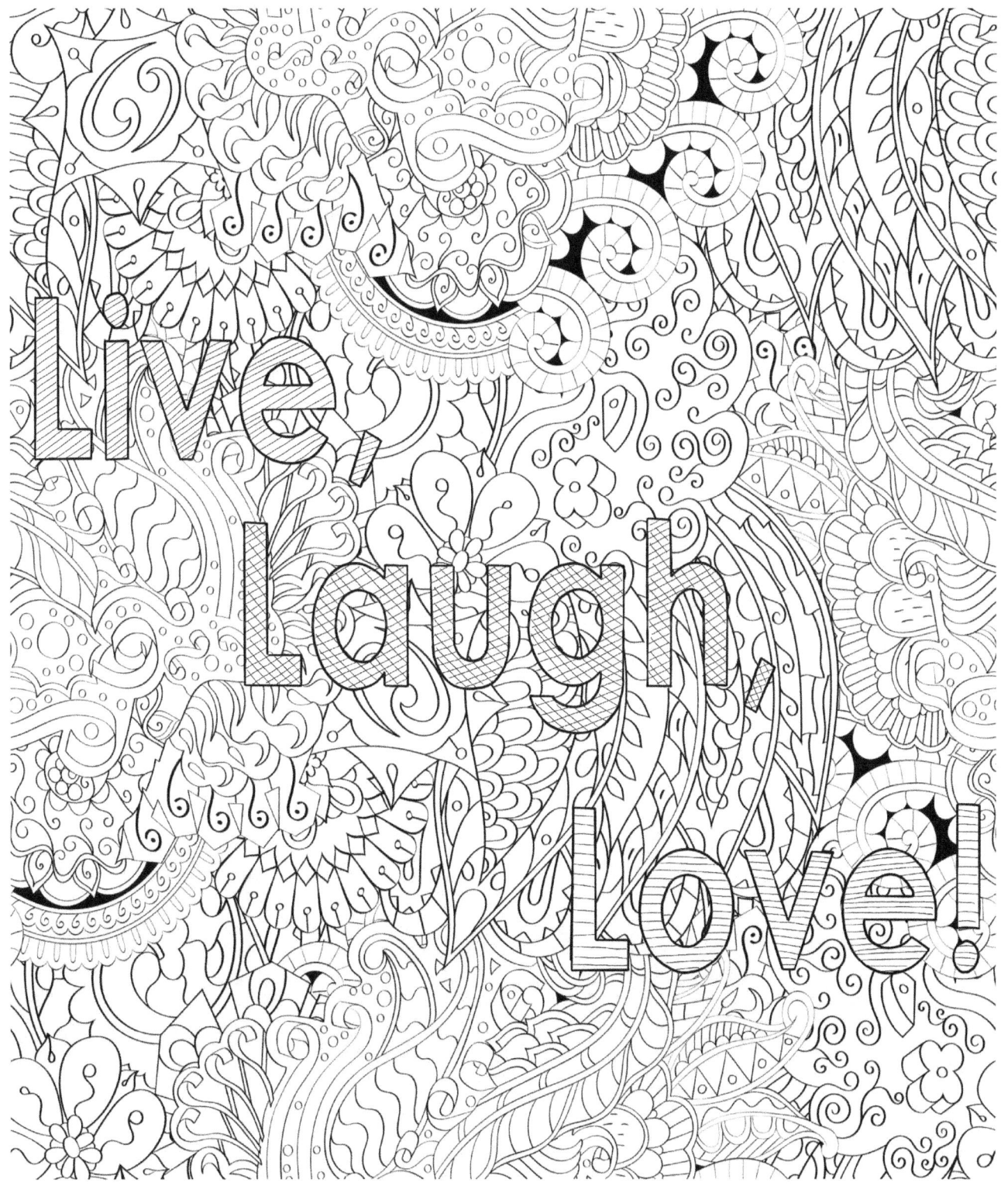

Everyone has at least one unstable friend,

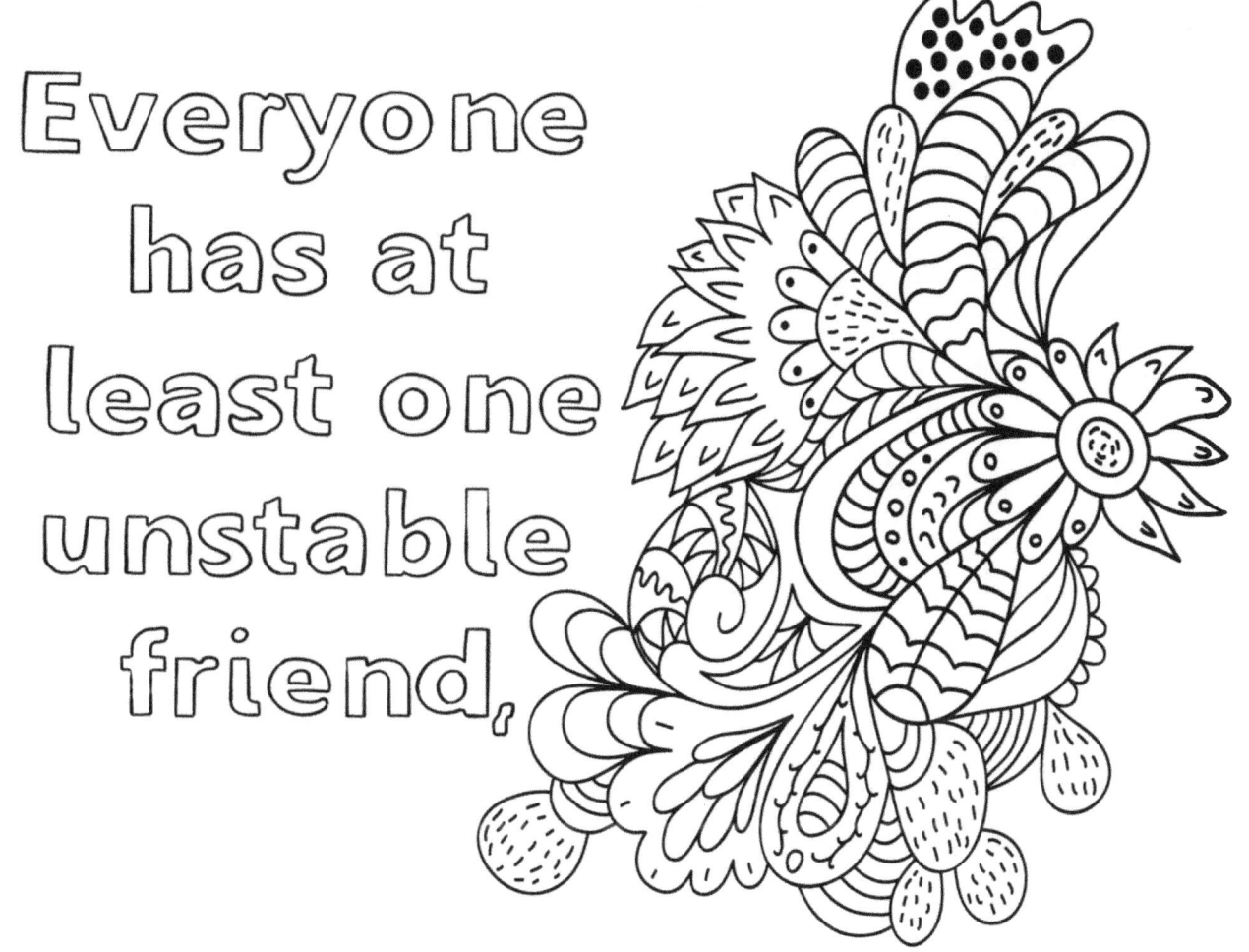

I just happen to be that friend!

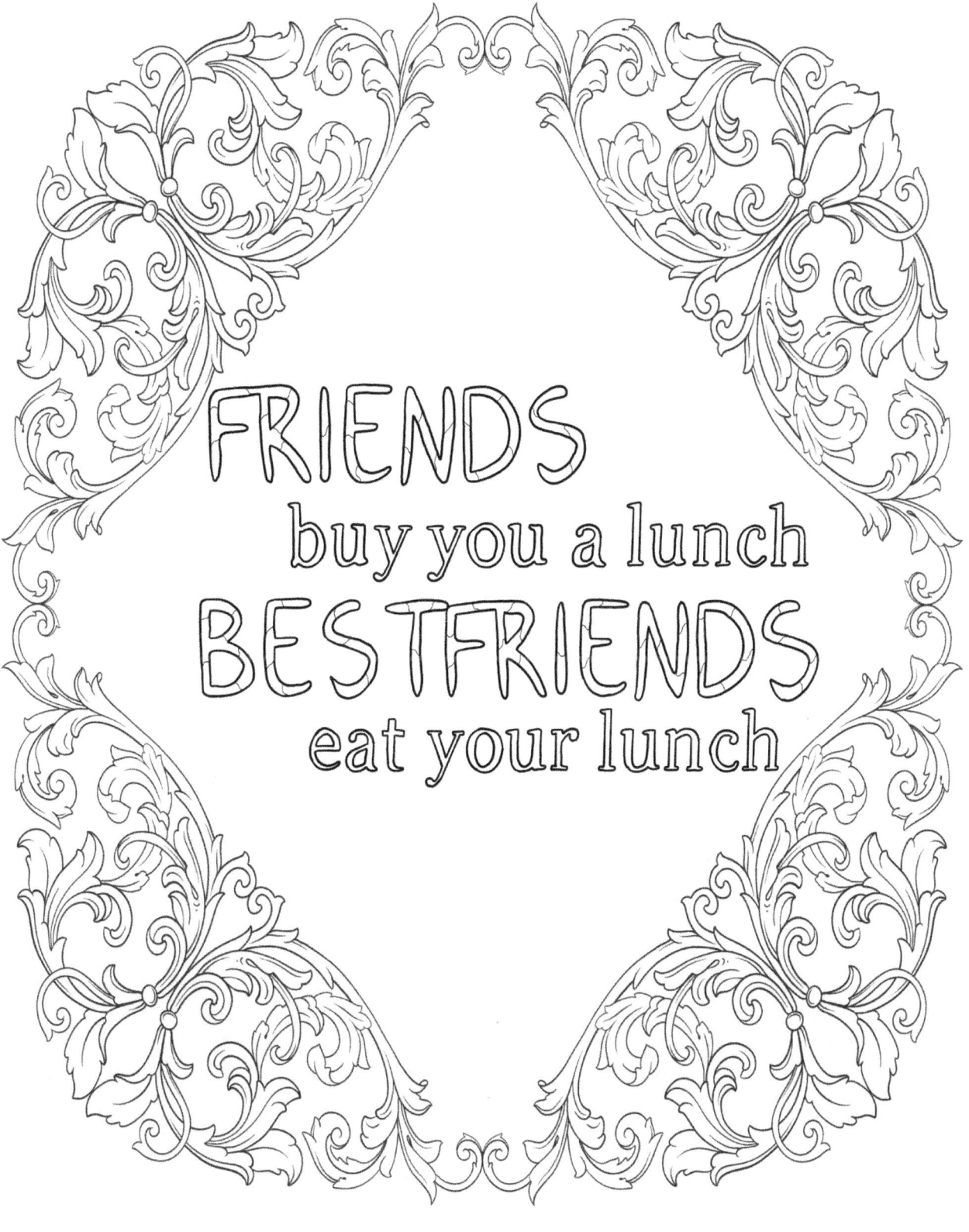

FRIENDS
buy you a lunch
BESTFRIENDS
eat your lunch

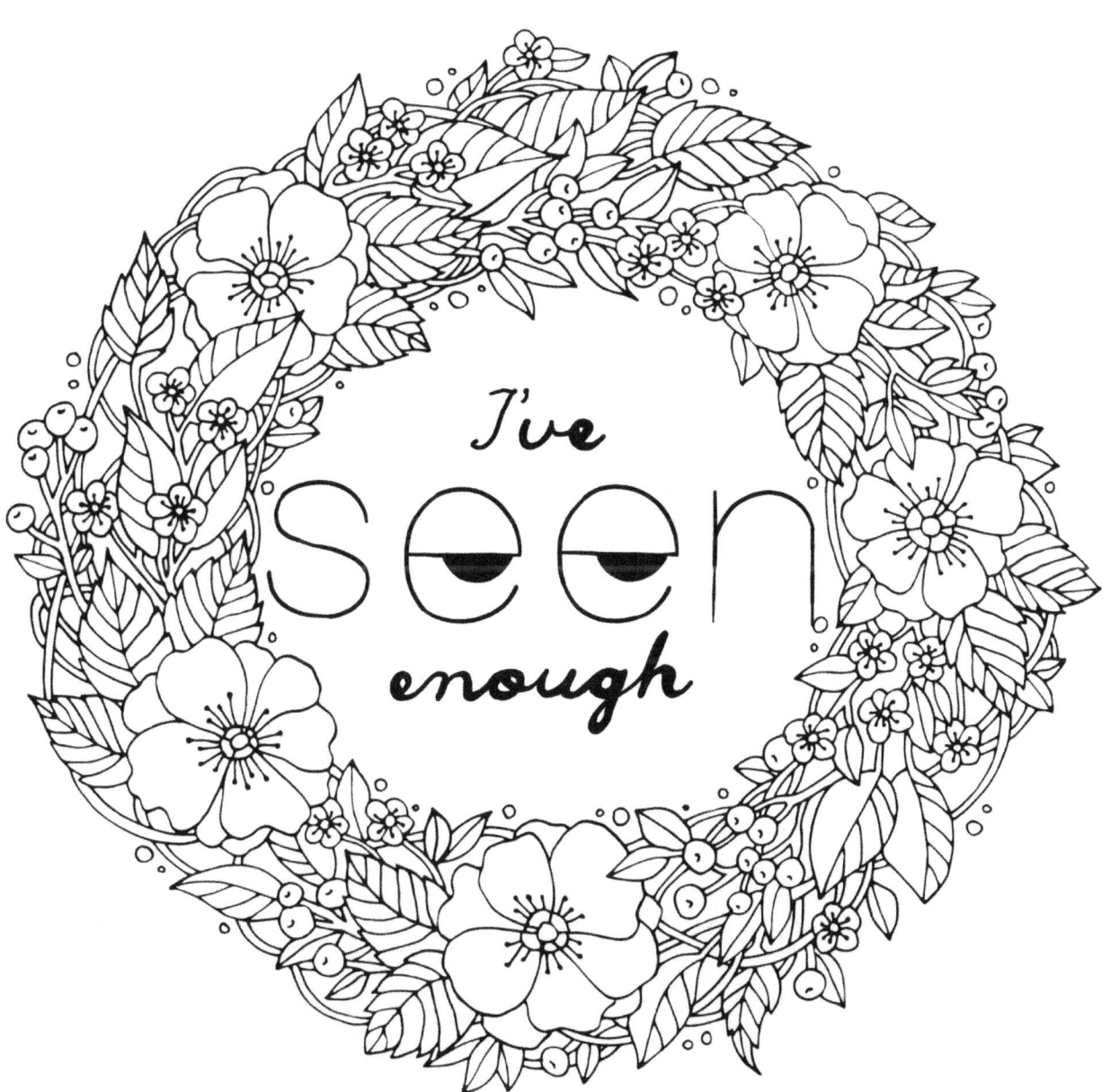

I've
seen
enough

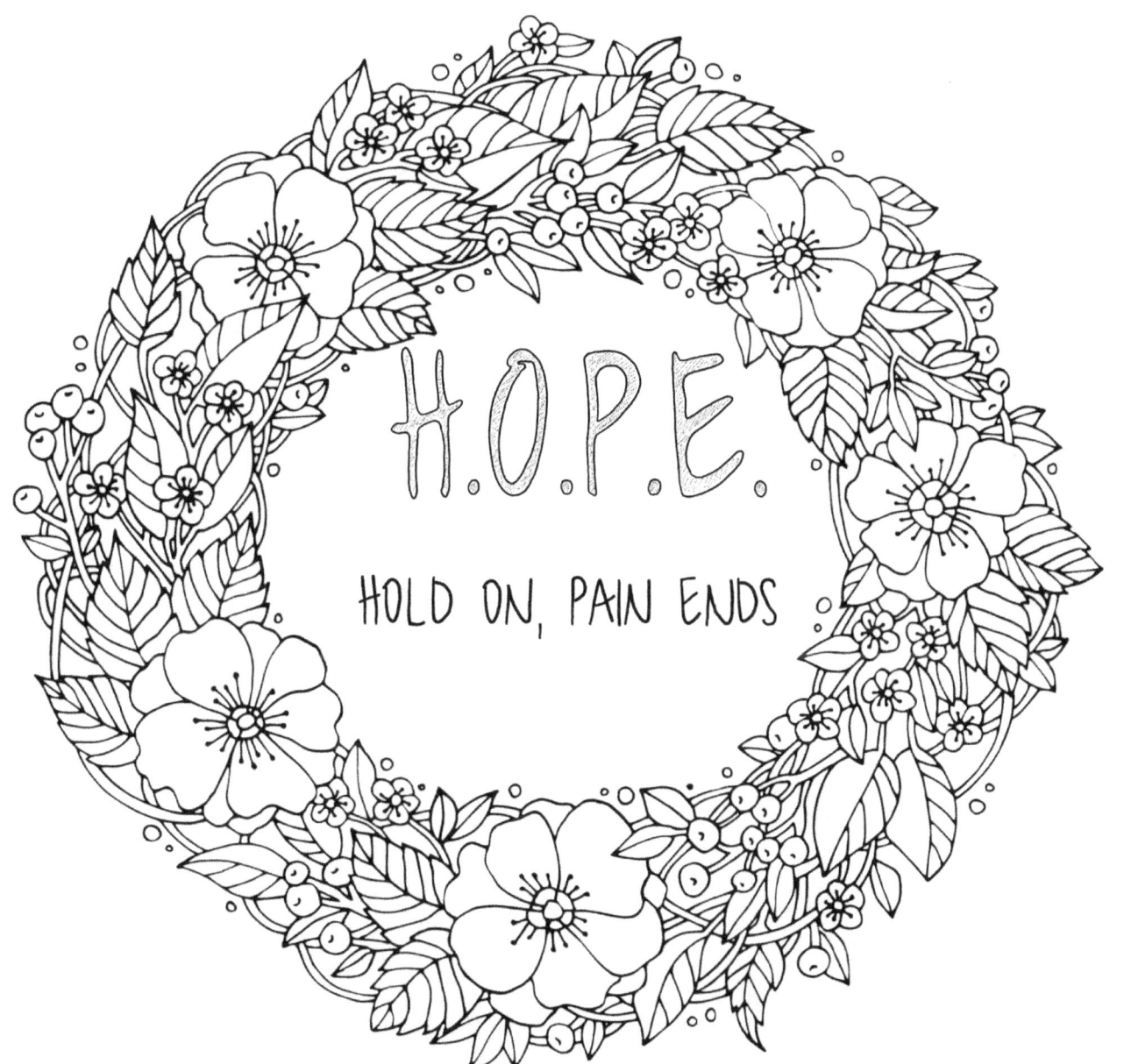

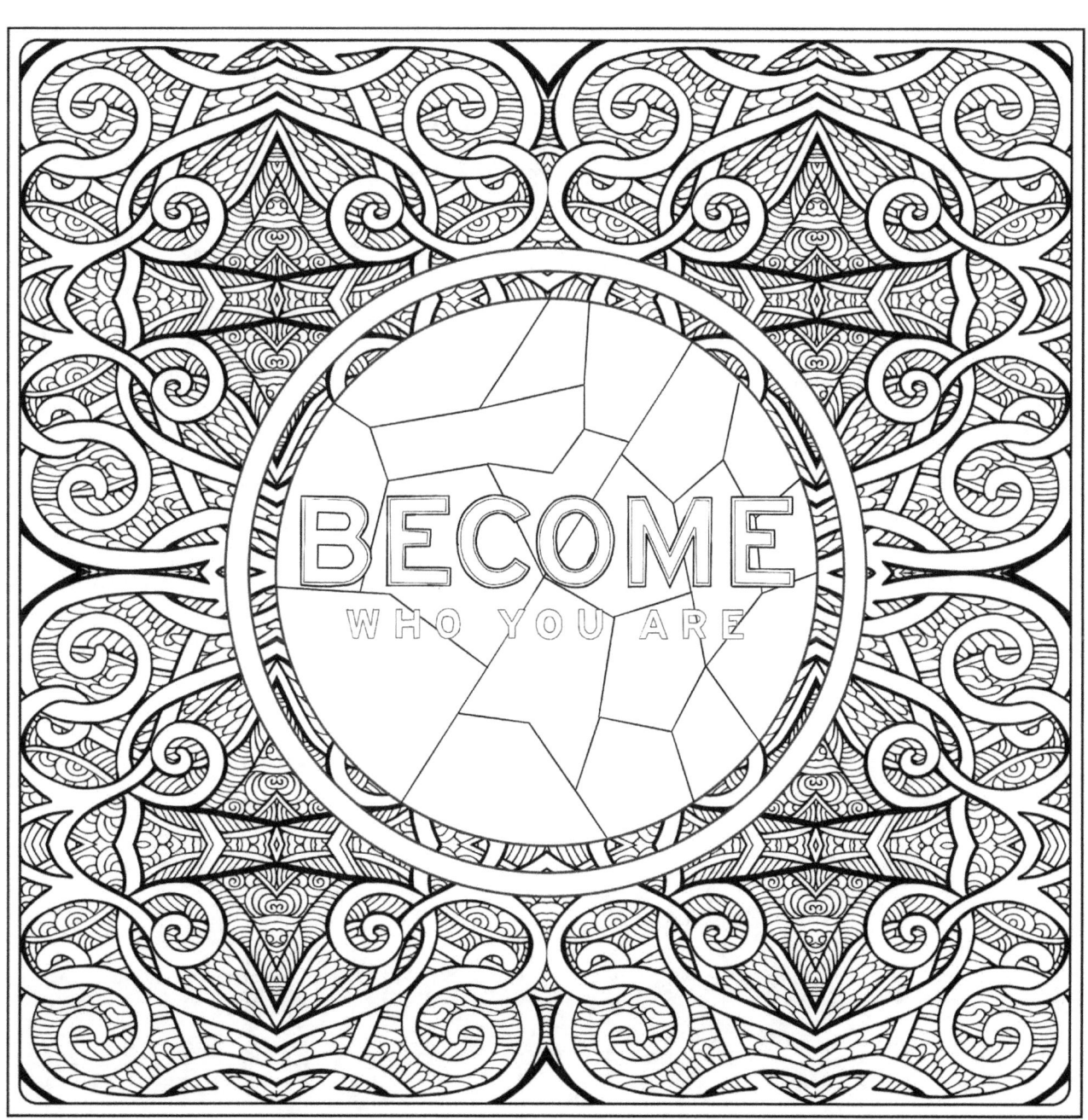

Different is Beautiful

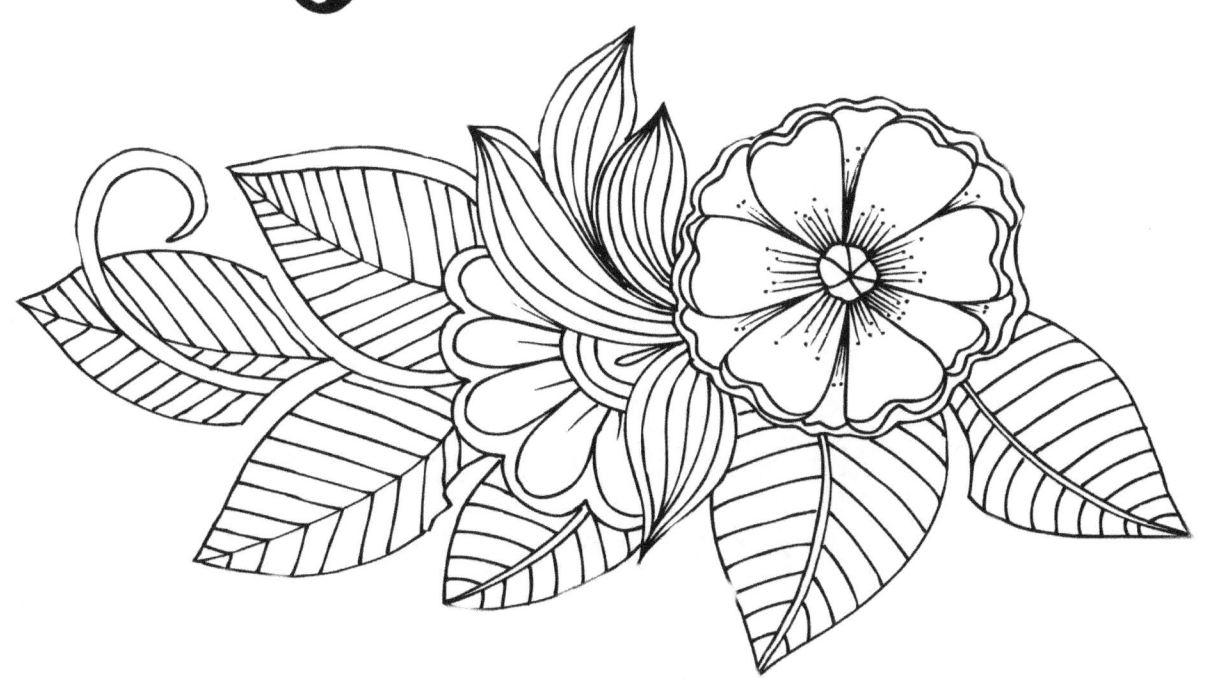

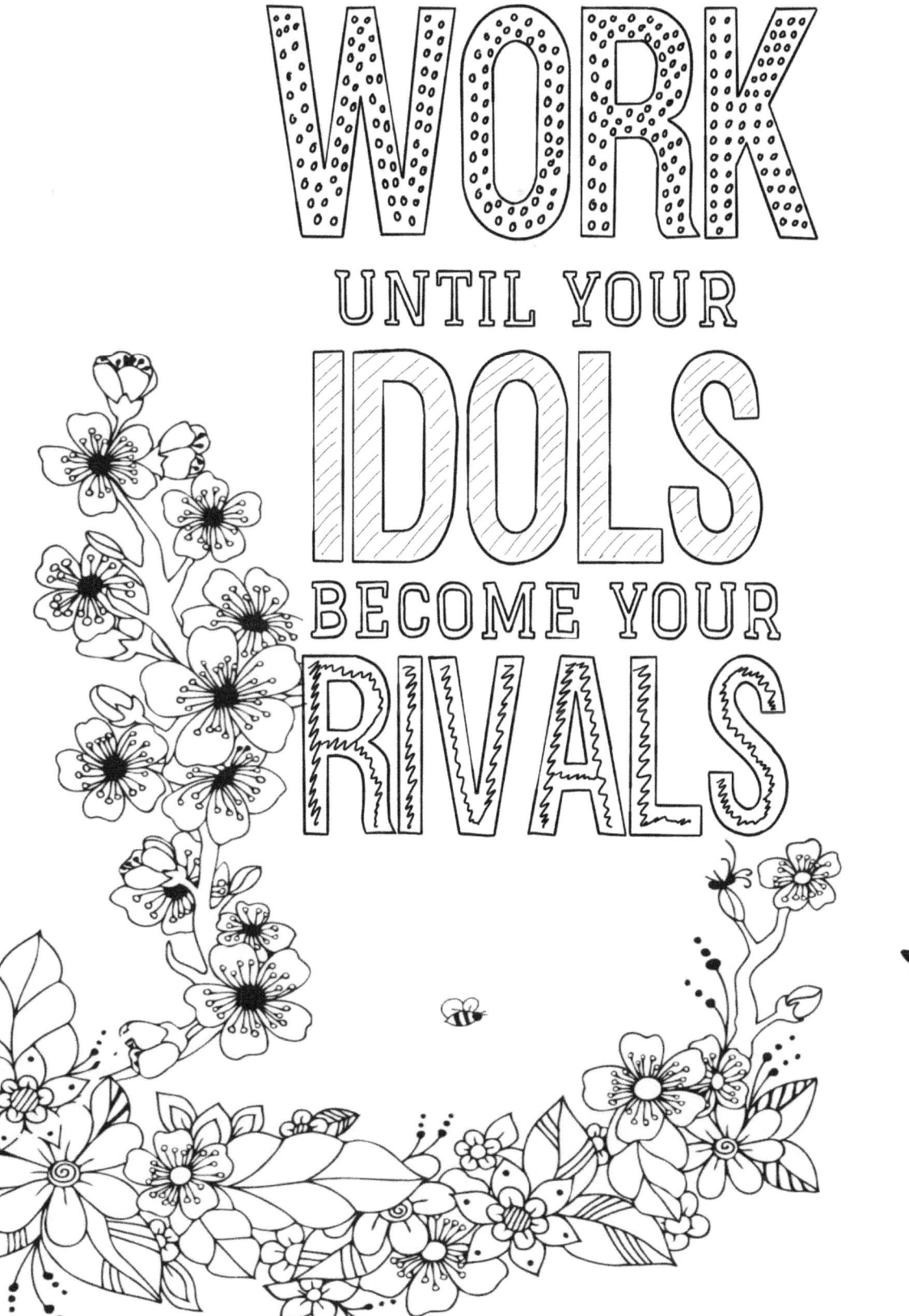

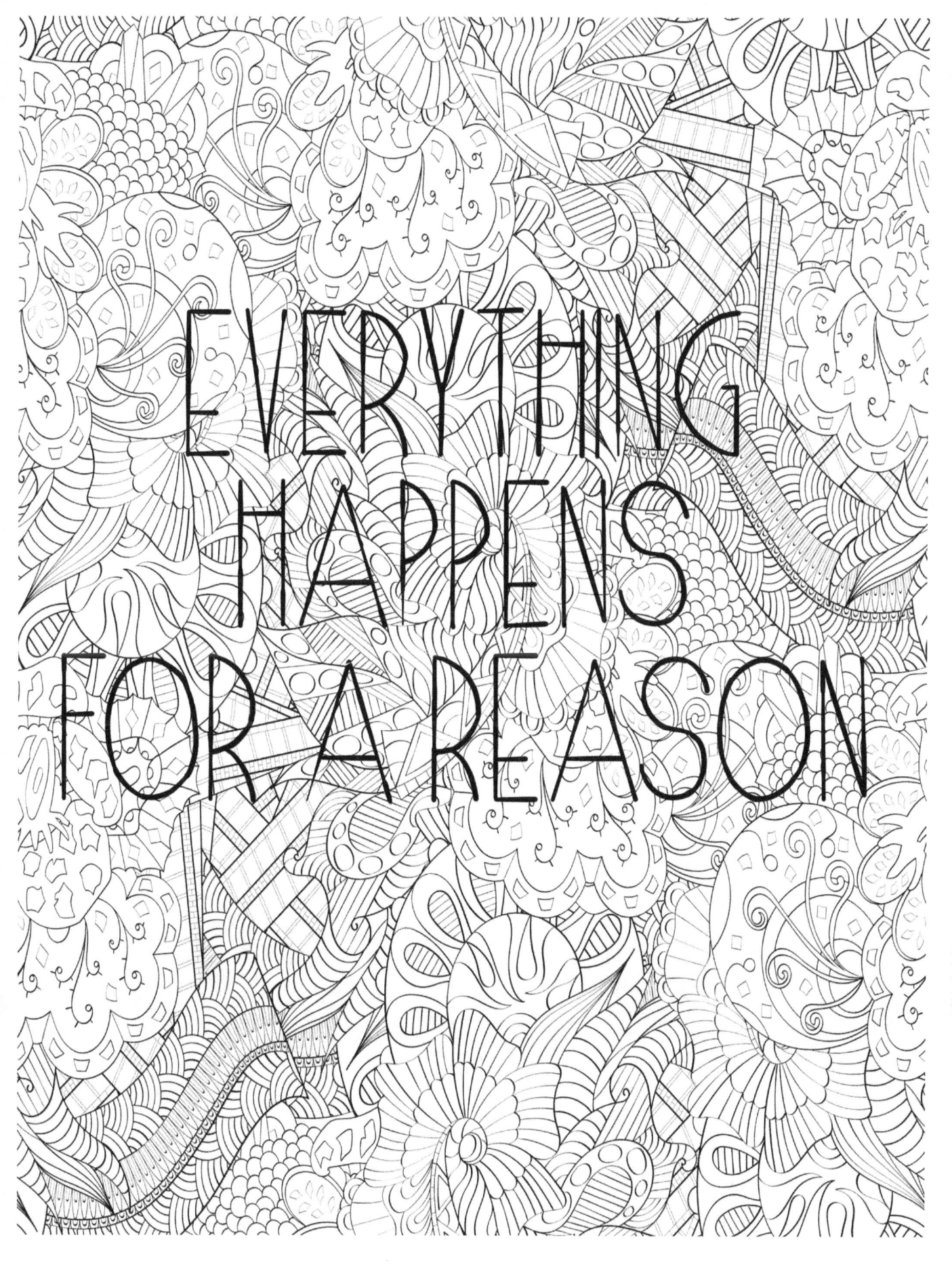

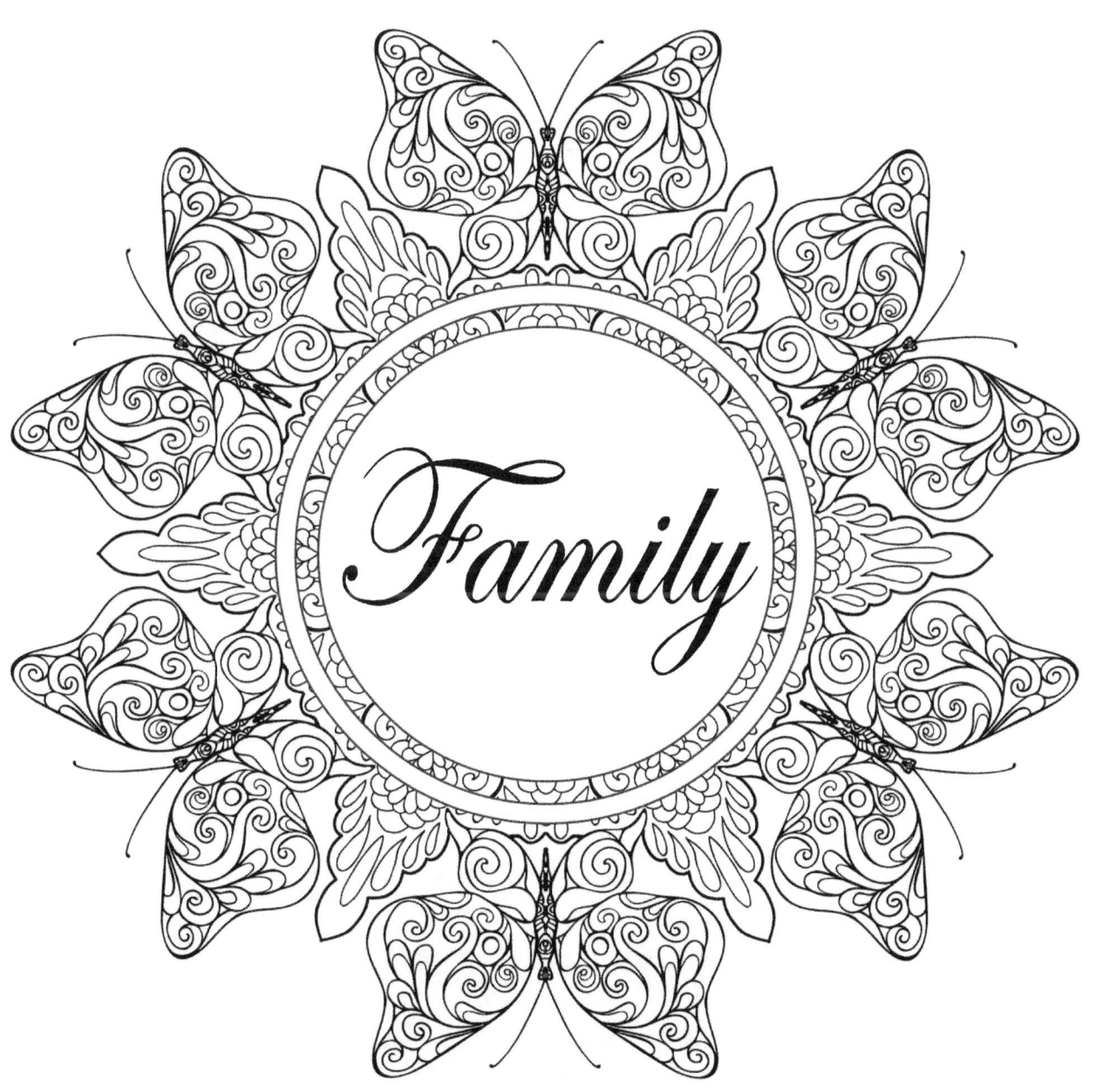

never let go of your
D R E A M S

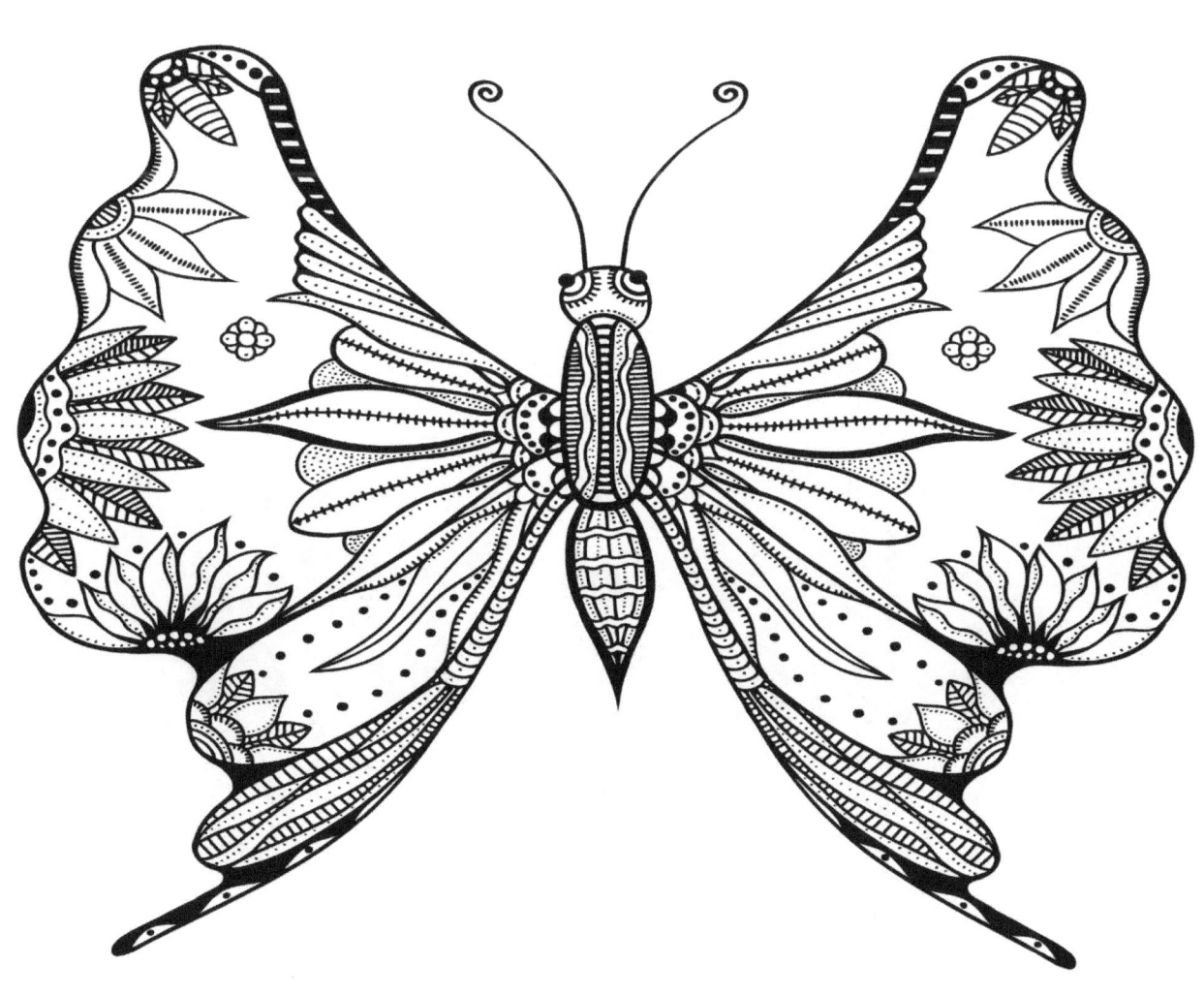

a good friend
knows all your best stories
a best friend
has lived them with you

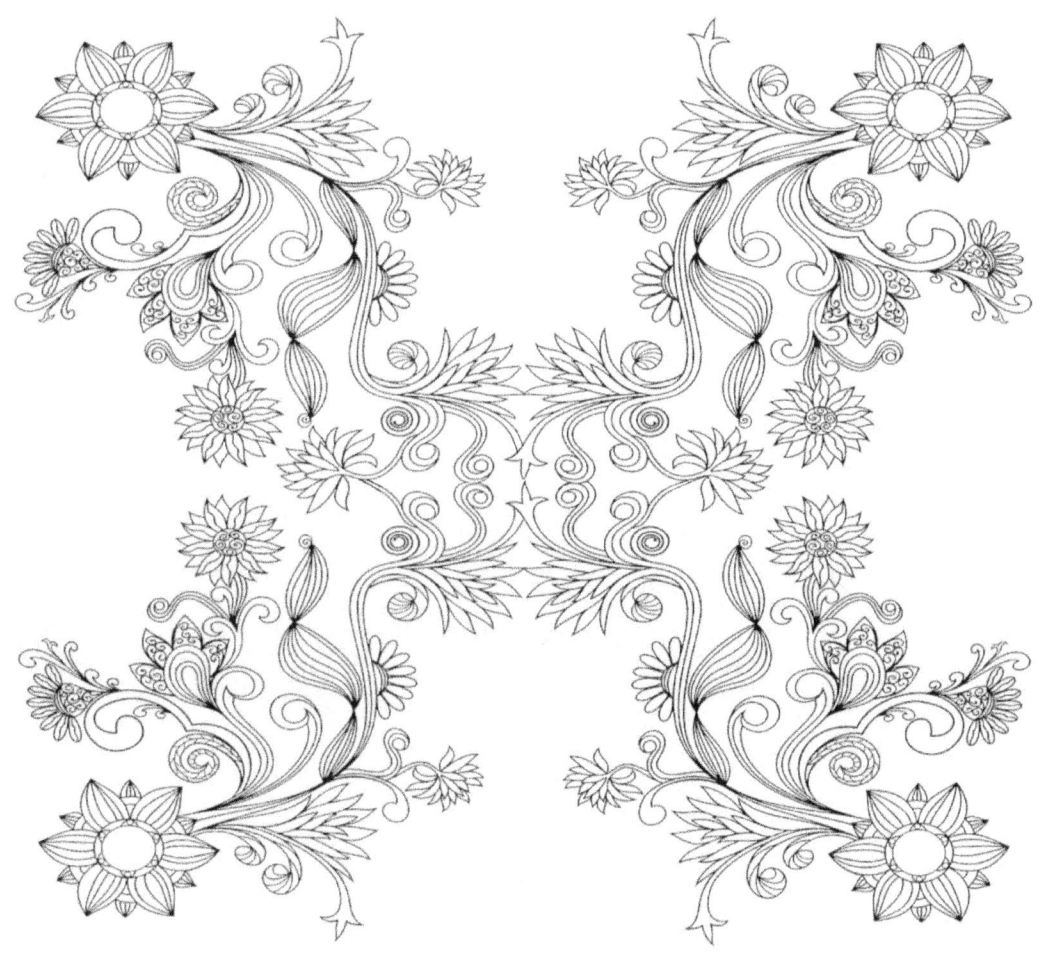

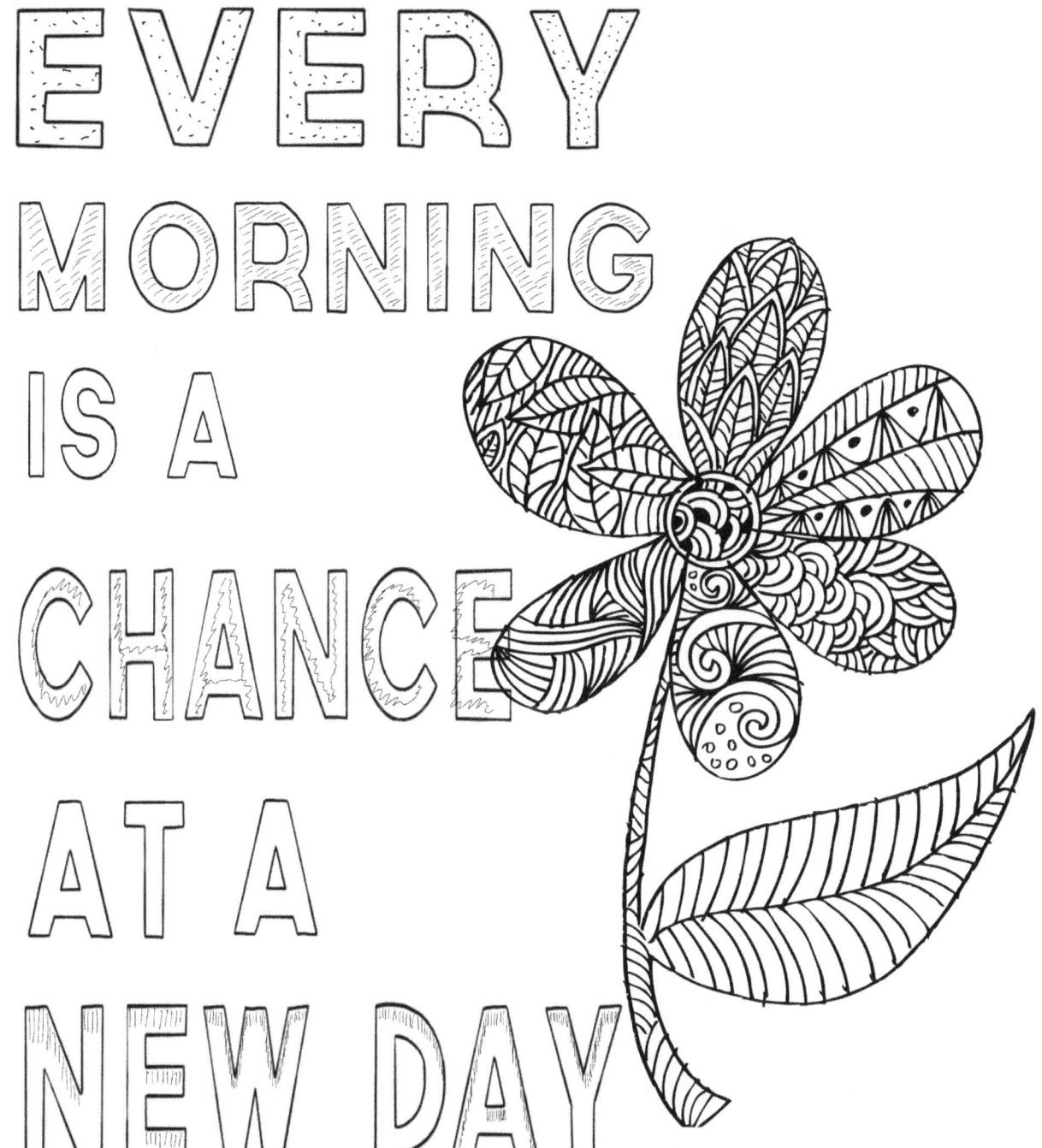

EVERY MORNING IS A CHANCE AT A NEW DAY

EXPECT NOTHING AND YOU WILL NEVER BE DISAPPOINTED

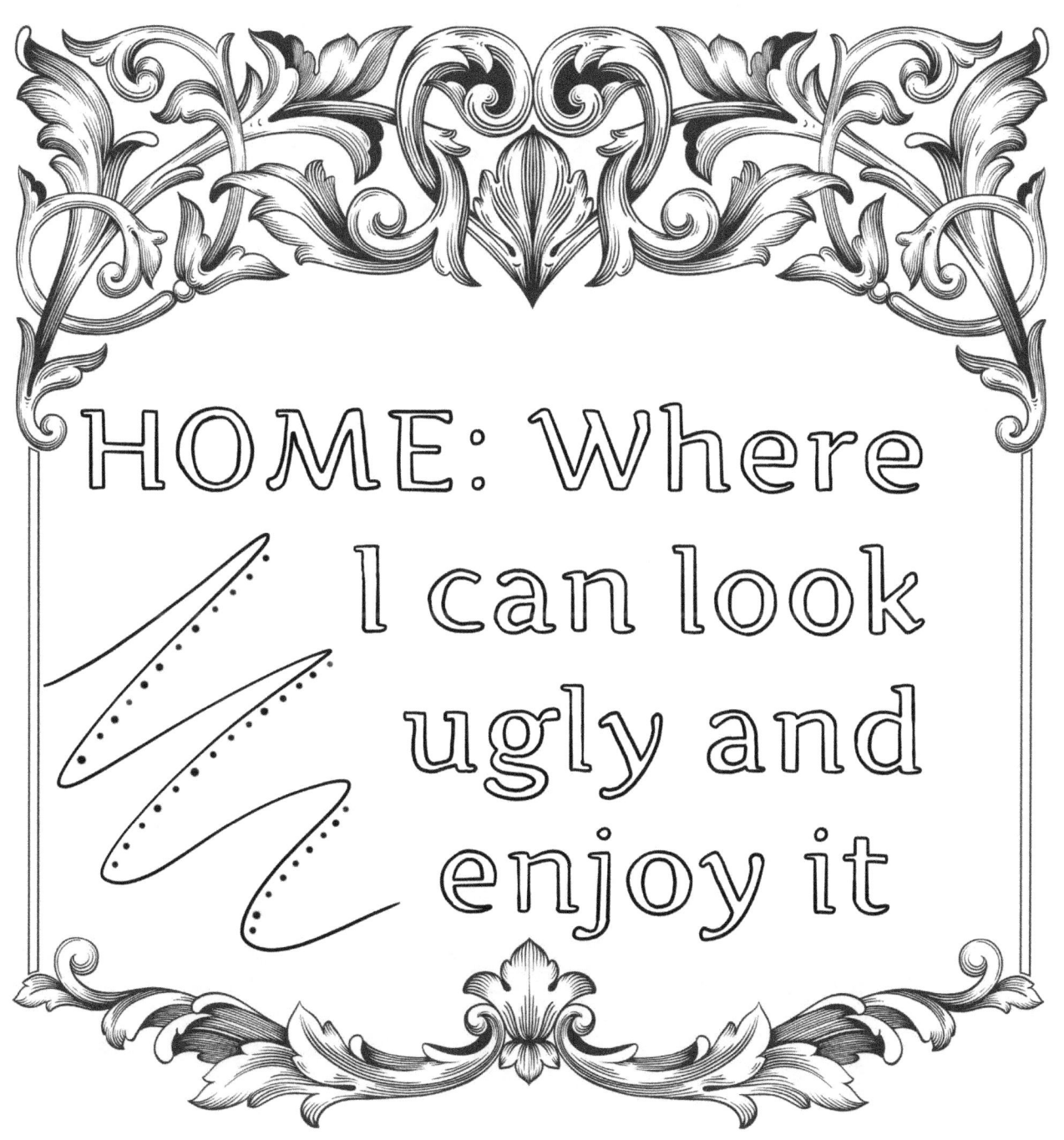

HOME: Where I can look ugly and enjoy it

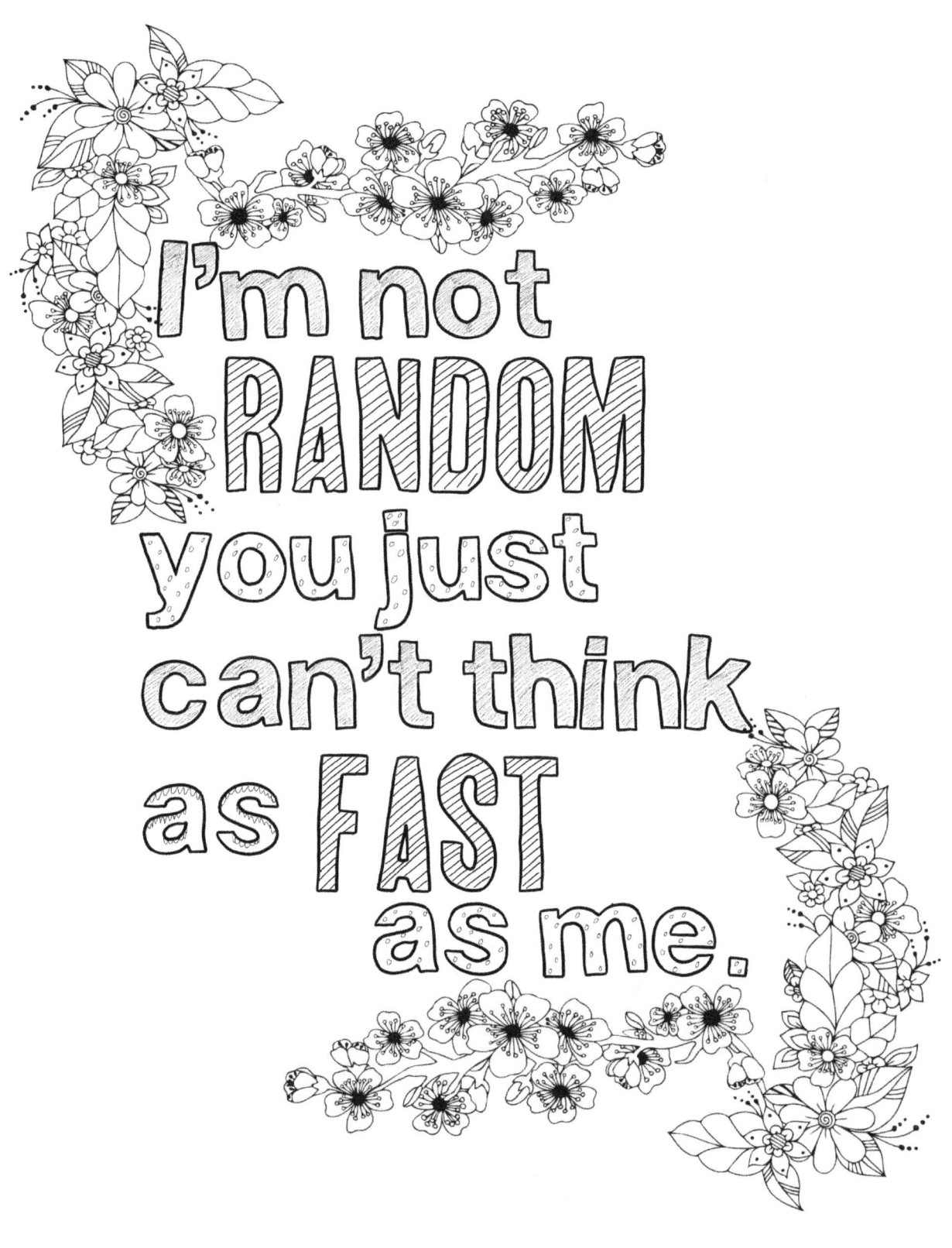

Don't find her
and lose yourself
Find yourself
to find her

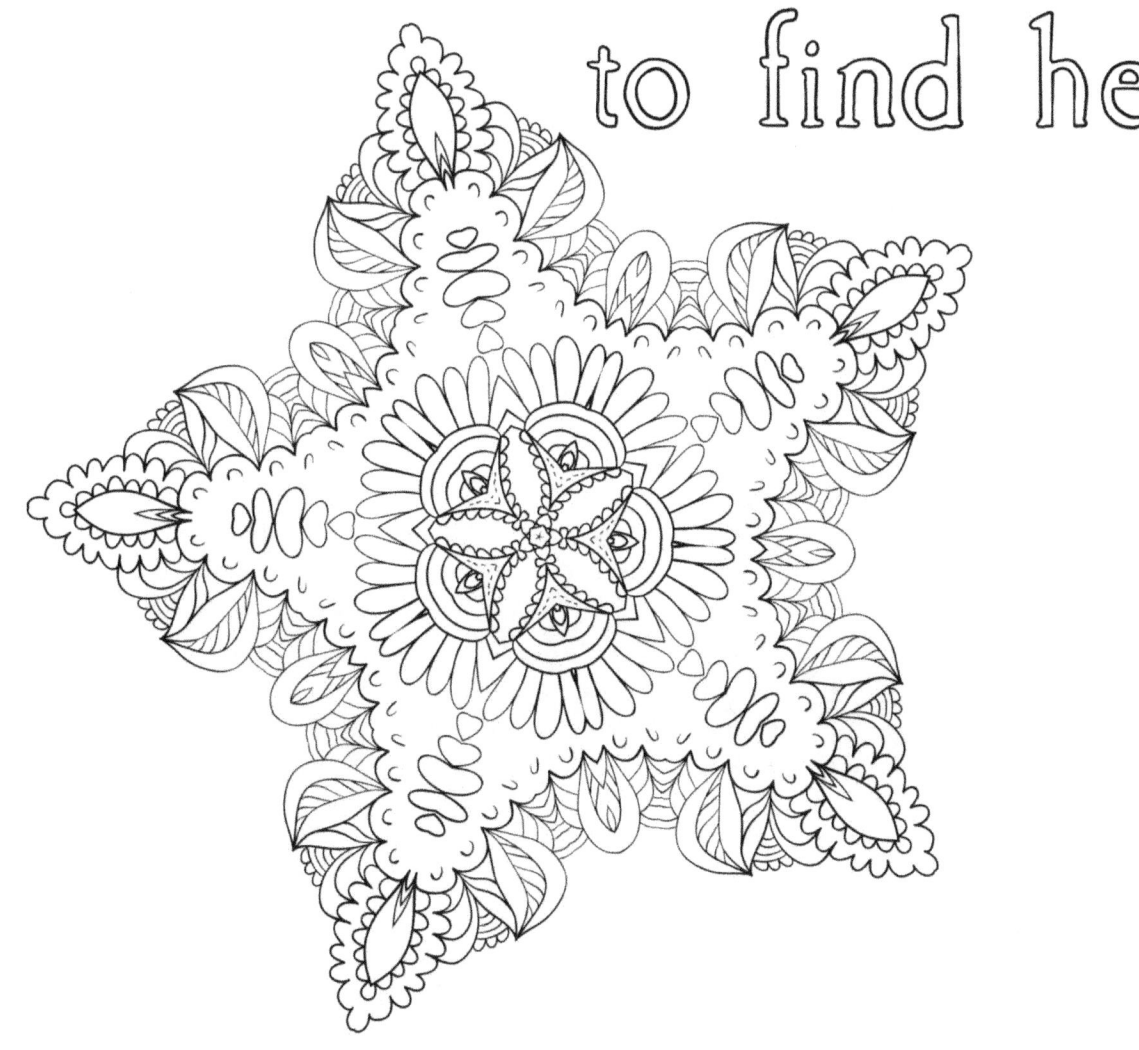

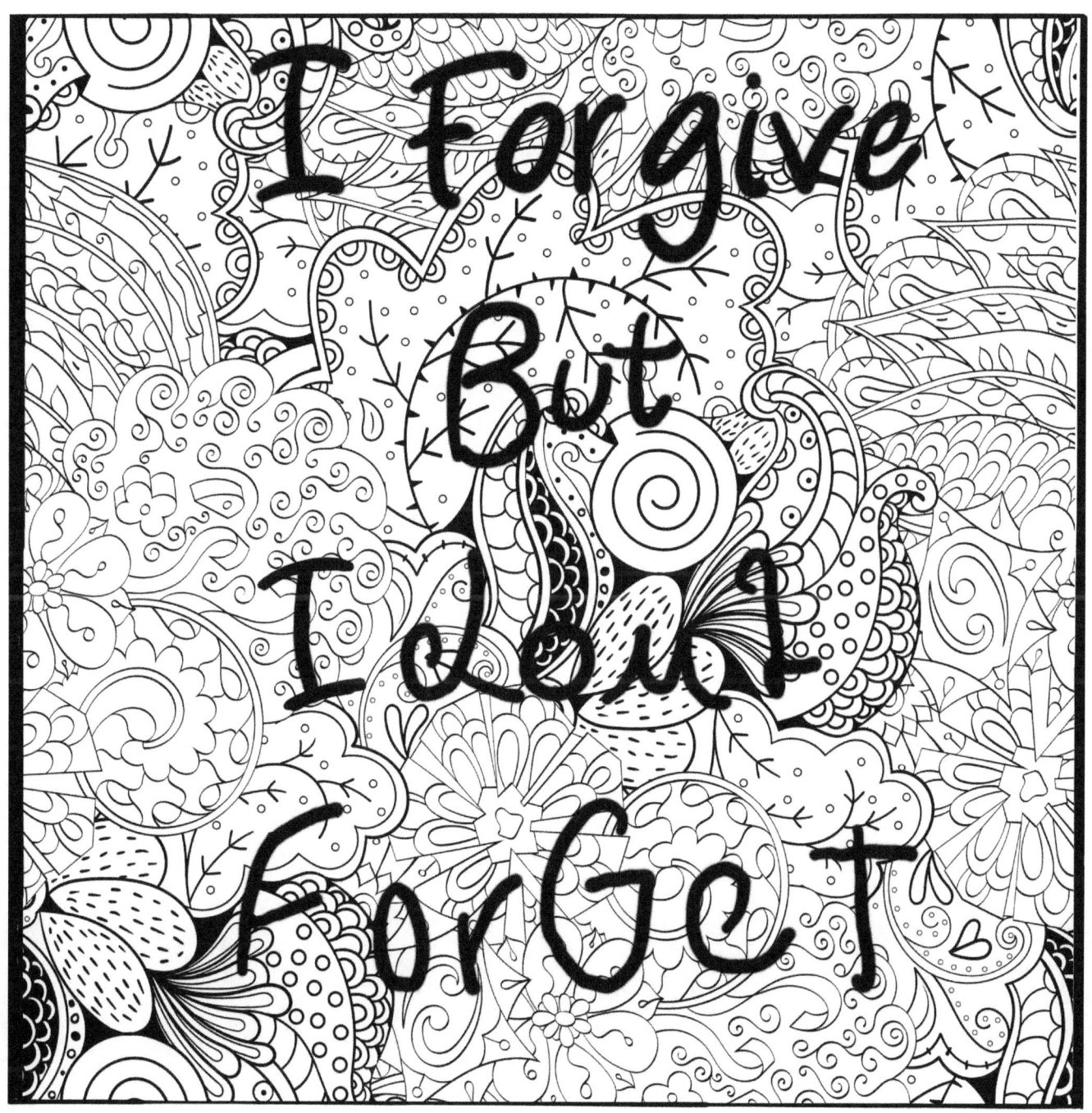

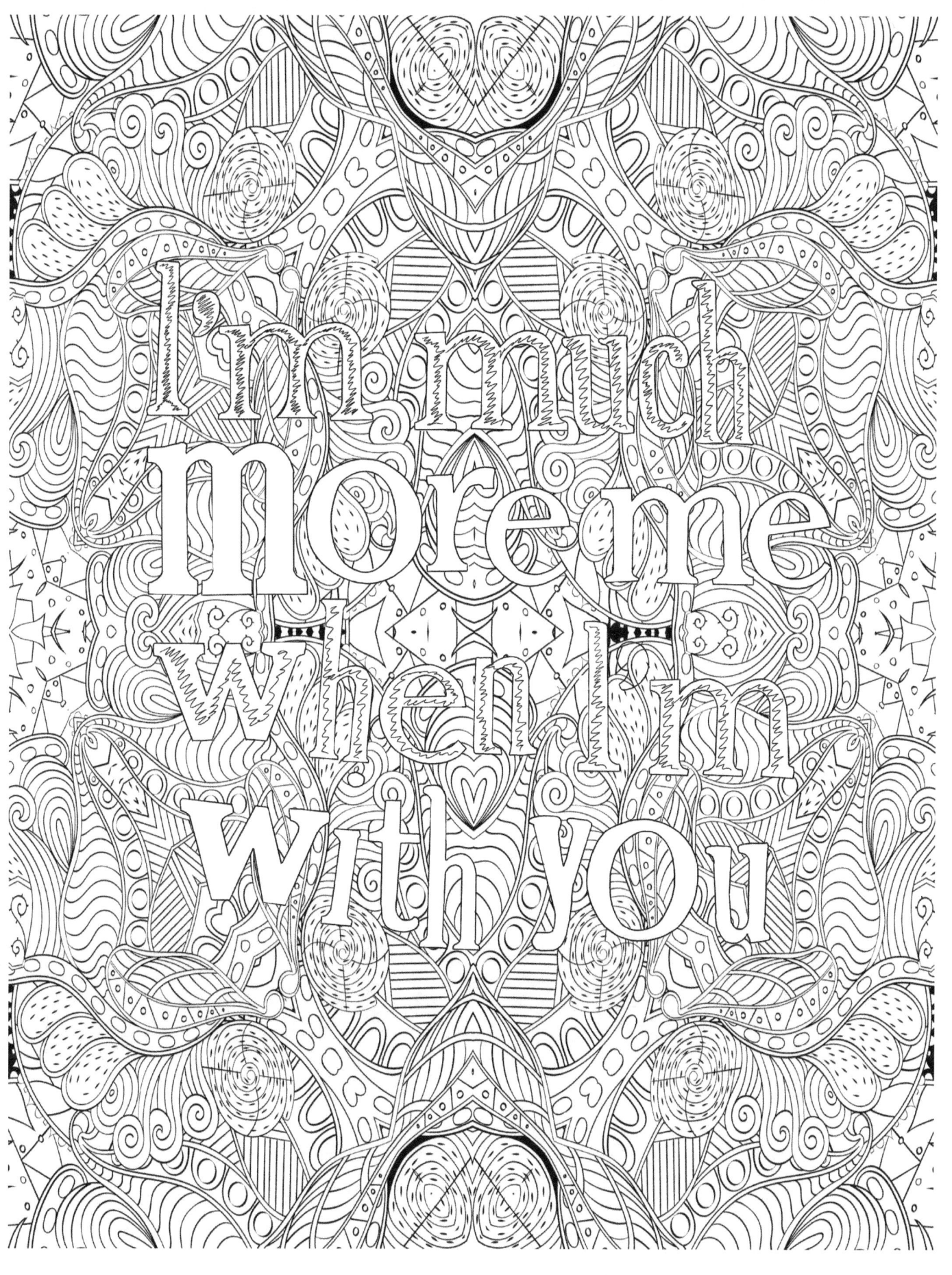